DISCARD

SUPERSIZED

Strange Tales from a Fast-Food Culture

SUPERSIZED
Strange Tales from a Fast-Food Culture

written by
Morgan Spurlock and **Jeremy Barlow**

art by
Lukas Ketner, Ron Chan, Lucas Marangon,
and **Tony Millionaire**

colors by
Ronda Pattison, Dan Jackson, and **Jim Campbell**

letters by
Michael David Thomas

cover by
Ron English

DARK HORSE BOOKS®

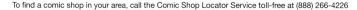

publisher • Mike Richardson
assistant editor • Patrick Thorpe
editor • Dave Land

[redacted]

Dark Horse Books
A division of Dark Horse Comics, Inc.
10956 SE Main Street
Milwaukie, OR 97222

darkhorse.com

To find a comic shop in your area, call the Comic Shop Locator Service toll-free at (888) 266-4226

First edition: April 2011
ISBN 978-1-59582-511-7

10 9 8 7 6 5 4 3 2 1
Printed by 1010 Printing International, Ltd., Guangdong Province, China.

SUPERSIZED: STRANGE TALES FROM A FAST-FOOD CULTURE

Table of Contents
Serving Size 1 Story / Servings per Container 30

INTRODUCTION

In the six years since *Super Size Me* premiered in theaters, I have been inundated with mind-blowing stories from people all around the world about weight loss, weight gain, fast-food manufacturing, the food's ingredients, and personal tell-all accounts about what *really* goes on behind the drive-thru windows.

I was fascinated and shocked by so many of these stories that I knew I had to find a way to get them out for the masses to read. That's when I met the great folks at Dark Horse Comics.

When I relayed some of the stories to the editors, they rolled around with as much laughter and disgust as I did, and thus *Supersized: Strange Tales from a Fast-Food Culture* was born.

Some of the stories were pulled from the original *Super Size Me* film, but the majority are brand-new accounts taken either from news organizations or the individuals themselves who actually worked on the frontlines of the fast-food battlegrounds.

With the help of the amazing Jeremy Barlow, Ron Chan, Lucas Marangon, Tony Millionaire, and Lukas Ketner, we crafted these exposés into the sometimes gross, sometimes educational, but always eye-opening book you now hold.

It's my hope that this is only the first volume of a series. After all, we've all had our own horrible food experiences that shouldn't be kept to ourselves. With the help of these books, you'll be able to share them with the world.

So, don't just sit there! Get reading! And then send us your story. You may actually see it in the sequel!

RealFastFoodStories@gmail.com

Happy eating!

—MORGAN SPURLOCK

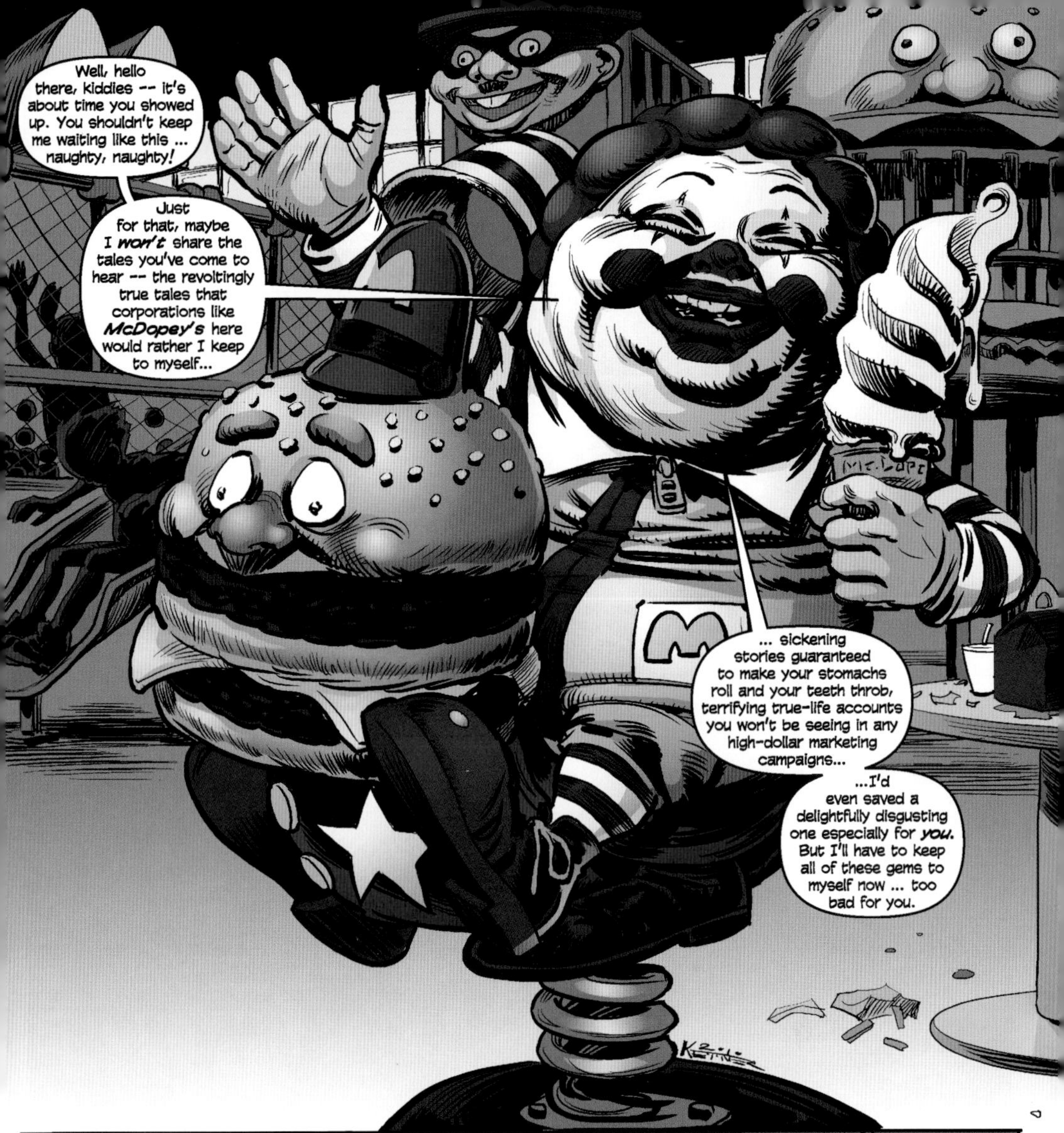
Well, hello there, kiddies -- it's about time you showed up. You shouldn't keep me waiting like this ... naughty, naughty!
Just for that, maybe I won't share the tales you've come to hear -- the revoltingly true tales that corporations like McDopey's here would rather I keep to myself...
... sickening stories guaranteed to make your stomachs roll and your teeth throb, terrifying true-life accounts you won't be seeing in any high-dollar marketing campaigns...
...I'd even saved a delightfully disgusting one especially for you. But I'll have to keep all of these gems to myself now ... too bad for you.

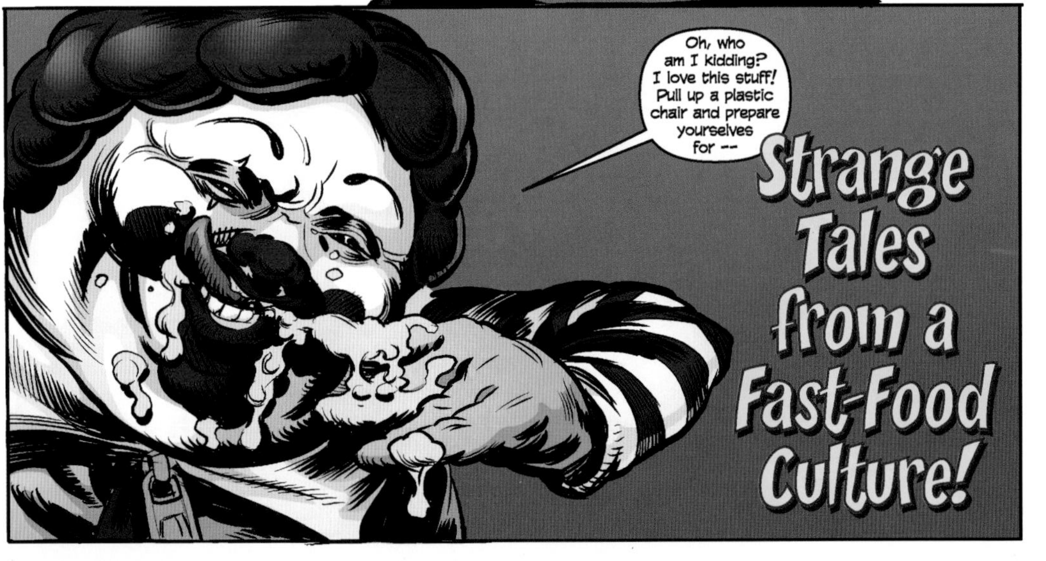
Oh, who am I kidding? I love this stuff! Pull up a plastic chair and prepare yourselves for --
Strange Tales from a Fast-Food Culture!

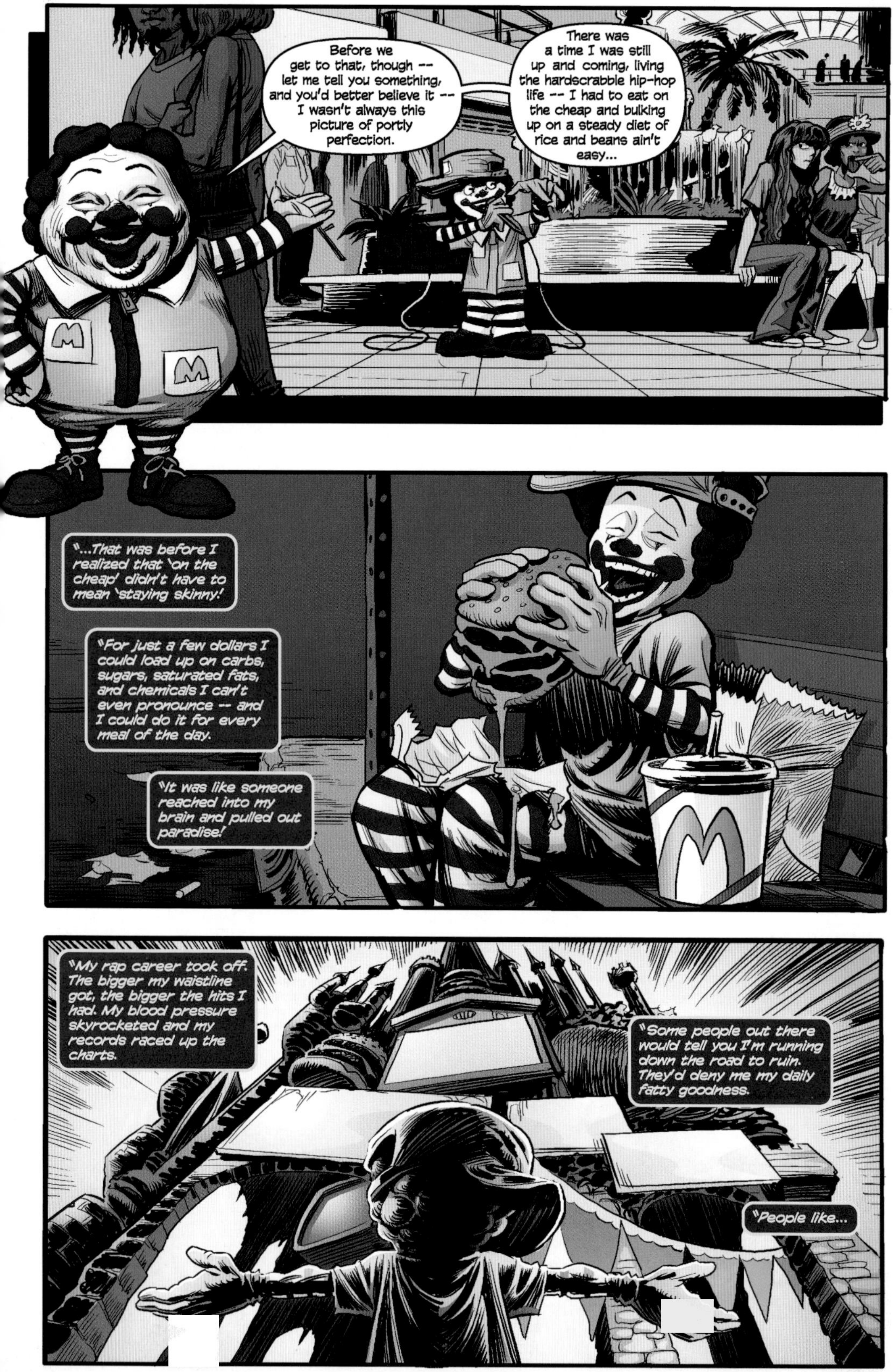
Before we get to that, though -- let me tell you something, and you'd better believe it -- I wasn't always this picture of portly perfection.
There was a time I was still up and coming, living the hardscrabble hip-hop life -- I had to eat on the cheap and bulking up on a steady diet of rice and beans ain't easy...
"...That was before I realized that 'on the cheap' didn't have to mean 'staying skinny.'
"For just a few dollars I could load up on carbs, sugars, saturated fats, and chemicals I can't even pronounce -- and I could do it for every meal of the day.
"It was like someone reached into my brain and pulled out paradise!
"My rap career took off. The bigger my waistline got, the bigger the hits I had. My blood pressure skyrocketed and my records raced up the charts.
"Some people out there would tell you I'm running down the road to ruin. They'd deny me my daily fatty goodness.
"People like...

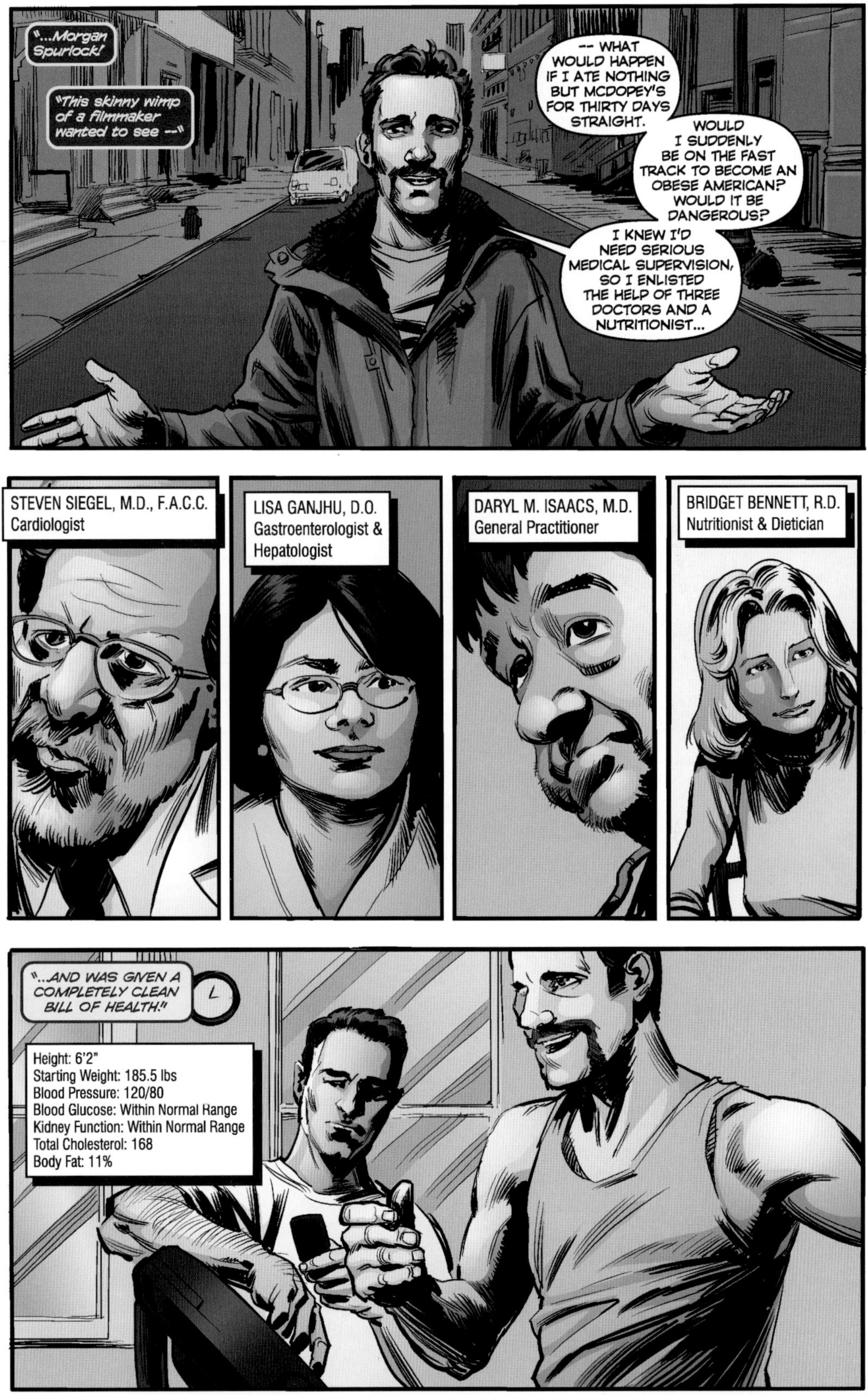
"...Morgan Spurlock!
"This skinny wimp of a filmmaker wanted to see --"
-- WHAT WOULD HAPPEN IF I ATE NOTHING BUT MCDOPEY'S FOR THIRTY DAYS STRAIGHT.
WOULD I SUDDENLY BE ON THE FAST TRACK TO BECOME AN OBESE AMERICAN? WOULD IT BE DANGEROUS?
I KNEW I'D NEED SERIOUS MEDICAL SUPERVISION, SO I ENLISTED THE HELP OF THREE DOCTORS AND A NUTRITIONIST...
STEVEN SIEGEL, M.D., F.A.C.C.
Cardiologist
LISA GANJHU, D.O.
Gastroenterologist & Hepatologist
DARYL M. ISAACS, M.D.
General Practitioner
BRIDGET BENNETT, R.D.
Nutritionist & Dietician
"...AND WAS GIVEN A COMPLETELY CLEAN BILL OF HEALTH."
Height: 6'2"
Starting Weight: 185.5 lbs
Blood Pressure: 120/80
Blood Glucose: Within Normal Range
Kidney Function: Within Normal Range
Total Cholesterol: 168
Body Fat: 11%

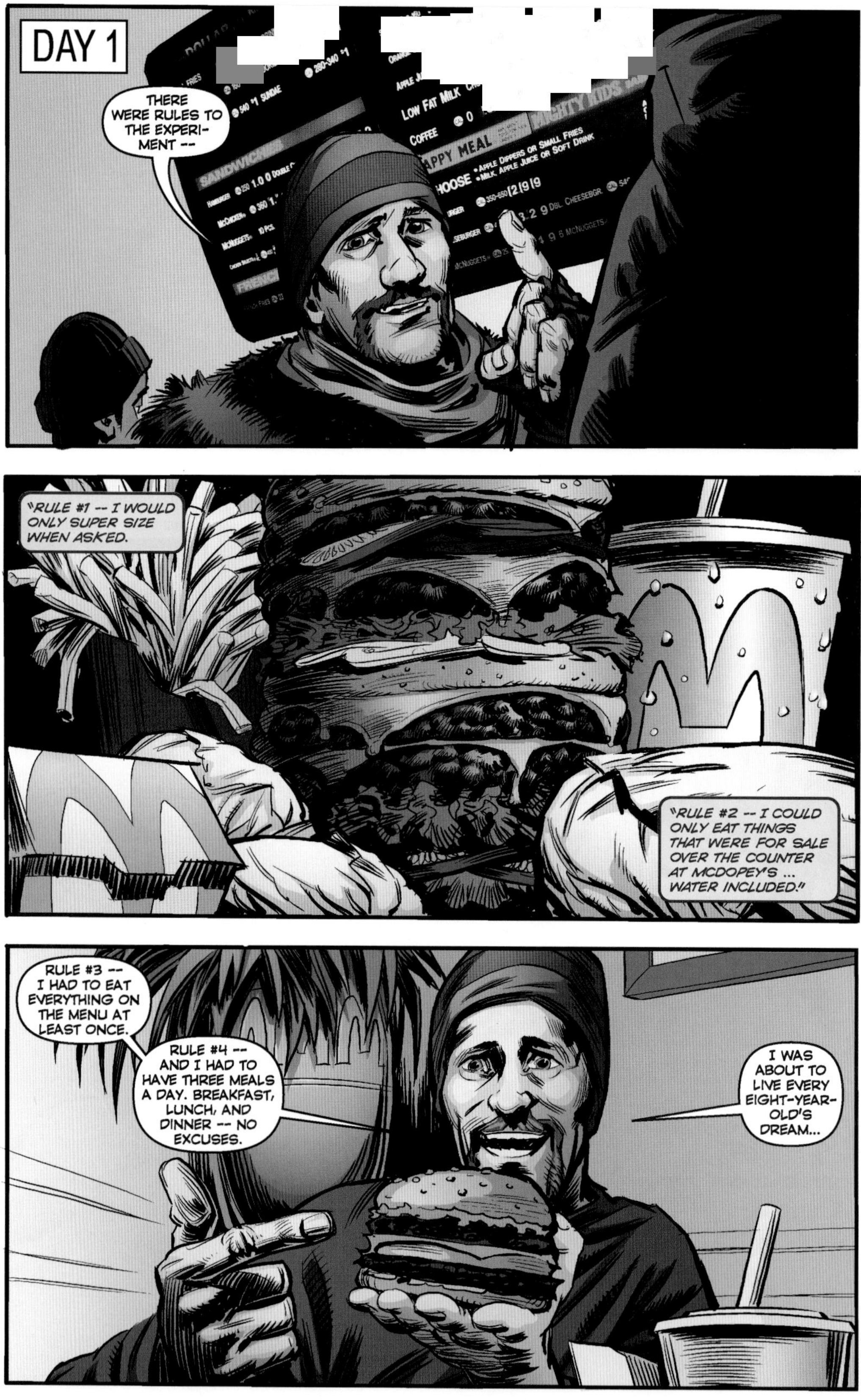
DAY 1
THERE WERE RULES TO THE EXPERI-MENT --
SANDWICHES
LOW FAT MILK
COFFEE
HAPPY MEAL
"RULE #1 -- I WOULD ONLY SUPER SIZE WHEN ASKED.
"RULE #2 -- I COULD ONLY EAT THINGS THAT WERE FOR SALE OVER THE COUNTER AT MCDOPEY'S ... WATER INCLUDED."
RULE #3 -- I HAD TO EAT EVERYTHING ON THE MENU AT LEAST ONCE.
RULE #4 -- AND I HAD TO HAVE THREE MEALS A DAY. BREAKFAST, LUNCH, AND DINNER -- NO EXCUSES.
I WAS ABOUT TO LIVE EVERY EIGHT-YEAR-OLD'S DREAM...

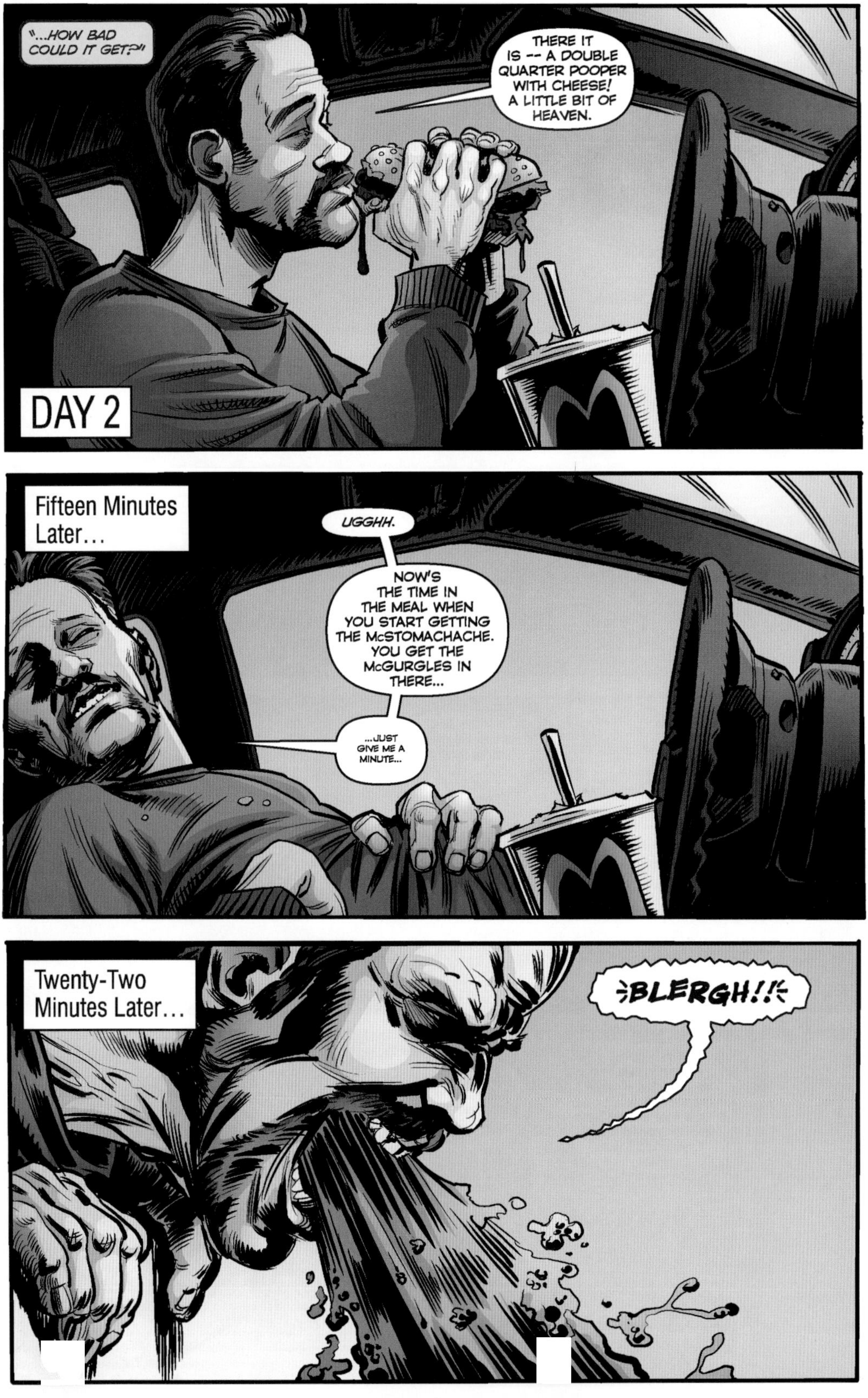
"...HOW BAD COULD IT GET?"
THERE IT IS -- A DOUBLE QUARTER POOPER WITH CHEESE! A LITTLE BIT OF HEAVEN.
DAY 2
Fifteen Minutes Later...
UGGHH.
NOW'S THE TIME IN THE MEAL WHEN YOU START GETTING THE McSTOMACHACHE. YOU GET THE McGURGLES IN THERE...
...JUST GIVE ME A MINUTE...
Twenty-Two Minutes Later...
BLERGH!!

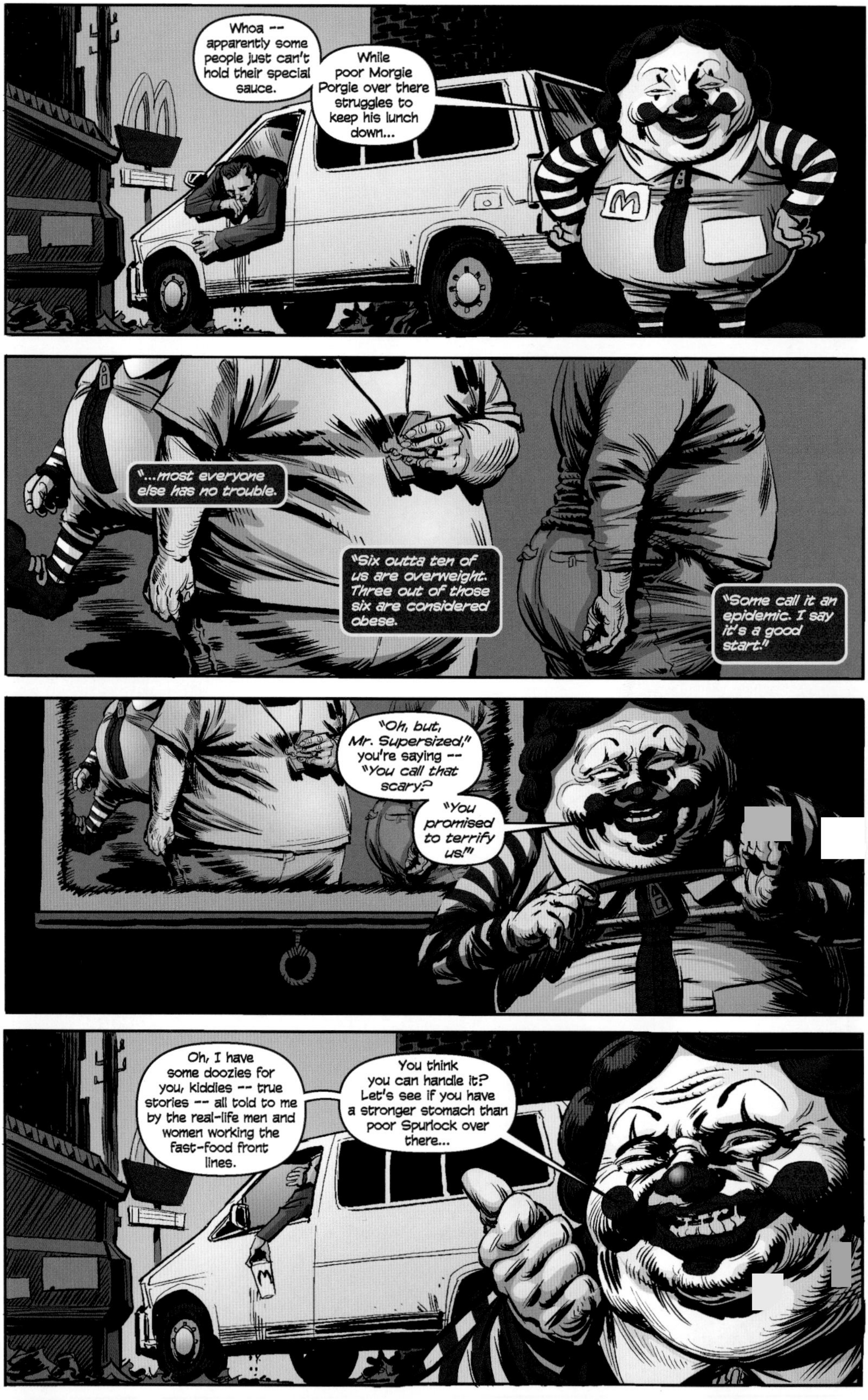

Whoa -- apparently some people just can't hold their special sauce.
While poor Morgie Porgie over there struggles to keep his lunch down...
"...most everyone else has no trouble.
"Six outta ten of us are overweight. Three out of those six are considered obese.
"Some call it an epidemic. I say it's a good start."
"Oh, but, Mr. Supersized," you're saying -- "You call that scary?
"You promised to terrify us!"
Oh, I have some doozies for you, kiddies -- true stories -- all told to me by the real-life men and women working the fast-food front lines.
You think you can handle it? Let's see if you have a stronger stomach than poor Spurlock over there...

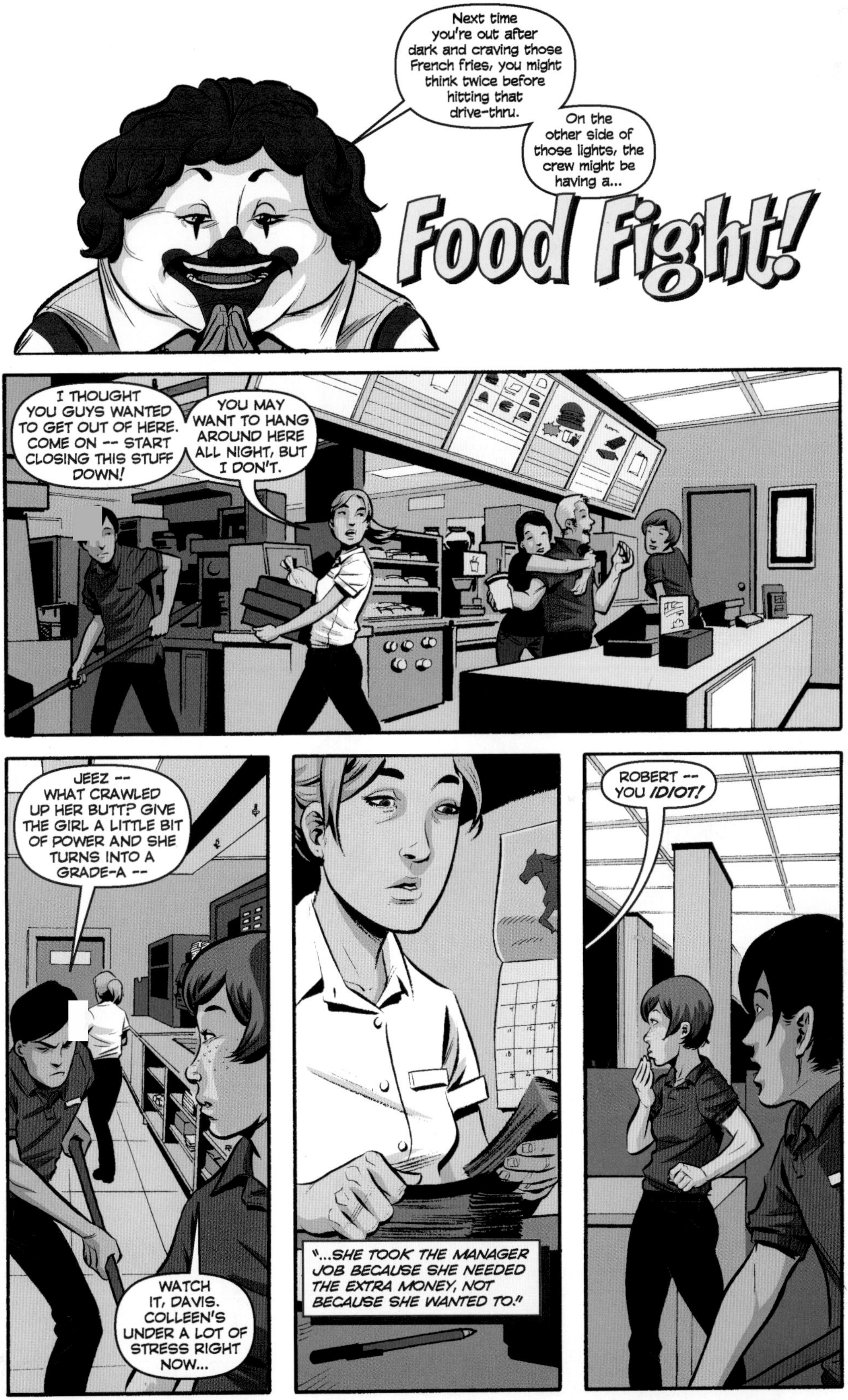
Next time you're out after dark and craving those French fries, you might think twice before hitting that drive-thru.
On the other side of those lights, the crew might be having a...
Food Fight!
I THOUGHT YOU GUYS WANTED TO GET OUT OF HERE. COME ON -- START CLOSING THIS STUFF DOWN!
YOU MAY WANT TO HANG AROUND HERE ALL NIGHT, BUT I DON'T.
JEEZ -- WHAT CRAWLED UP HER BUTT? GIVE THE GIRL A LITTLE BIT OF POWER AND SHE TURNS INTO A GRADE-A --
WATCH IT, DAVIS. COLLEEN'S UNDER A LOT OF STRESS RIGHT NOW...
"...SHE TOOK THE MANAGER JOB BECAUSE SHE NEEDED THE EXTRA MONEY, NOT BECAUSE SHE WANTED TO."
ROBERT -- YOU IDIOT!

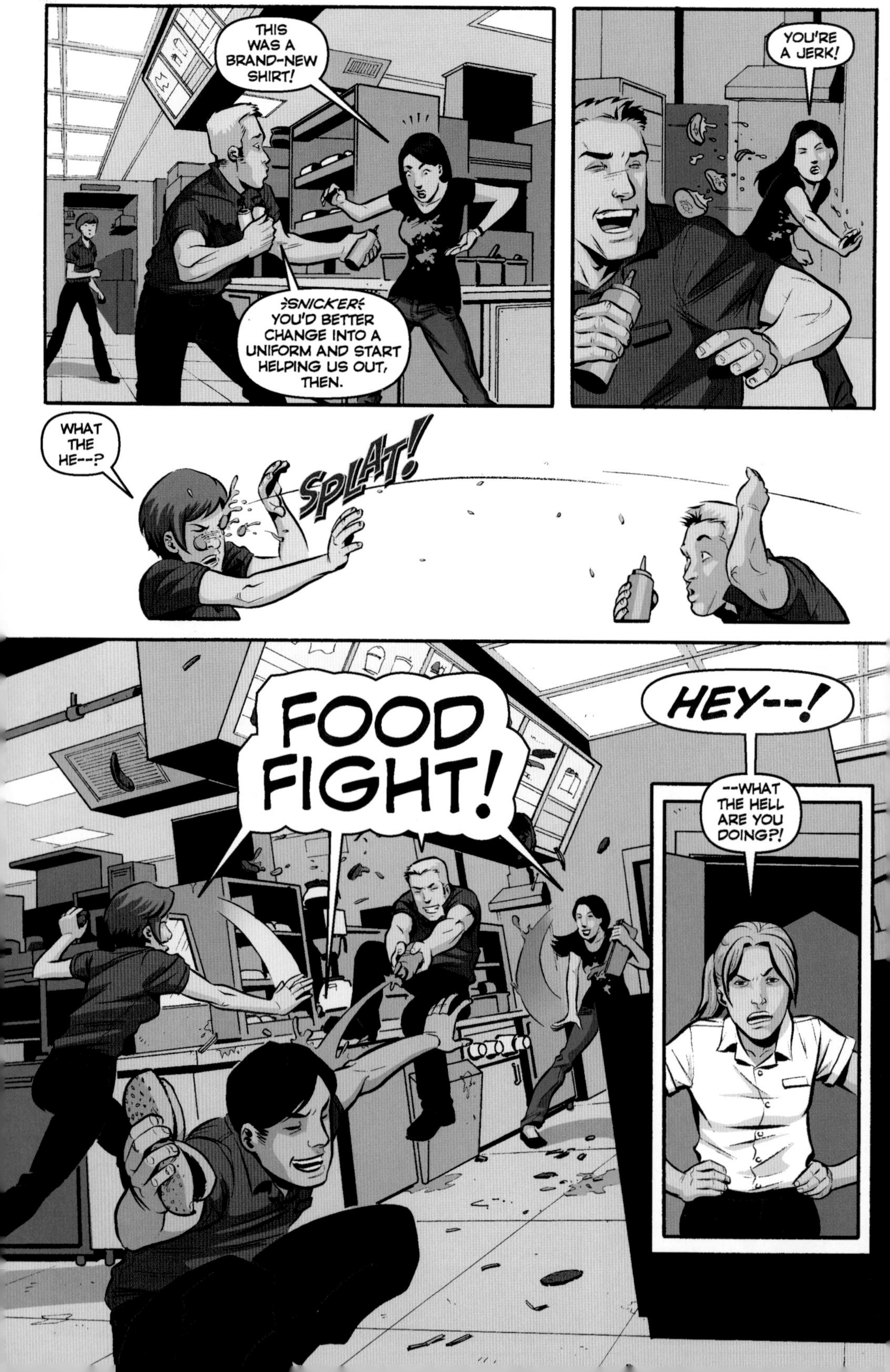
THIS WAS A BRAND-NEW SHIRT!
SNICKER YOU'D BETTER CHANGE INTO A UNIFORM AND START HELPING US OUT, THEN.
YOU'RE A JERK!
WHAT THE HE--?
SPLAT!
FOOD FIGHT!
HEY--!
--WHAT THE HELL ARE YOU DOING?!

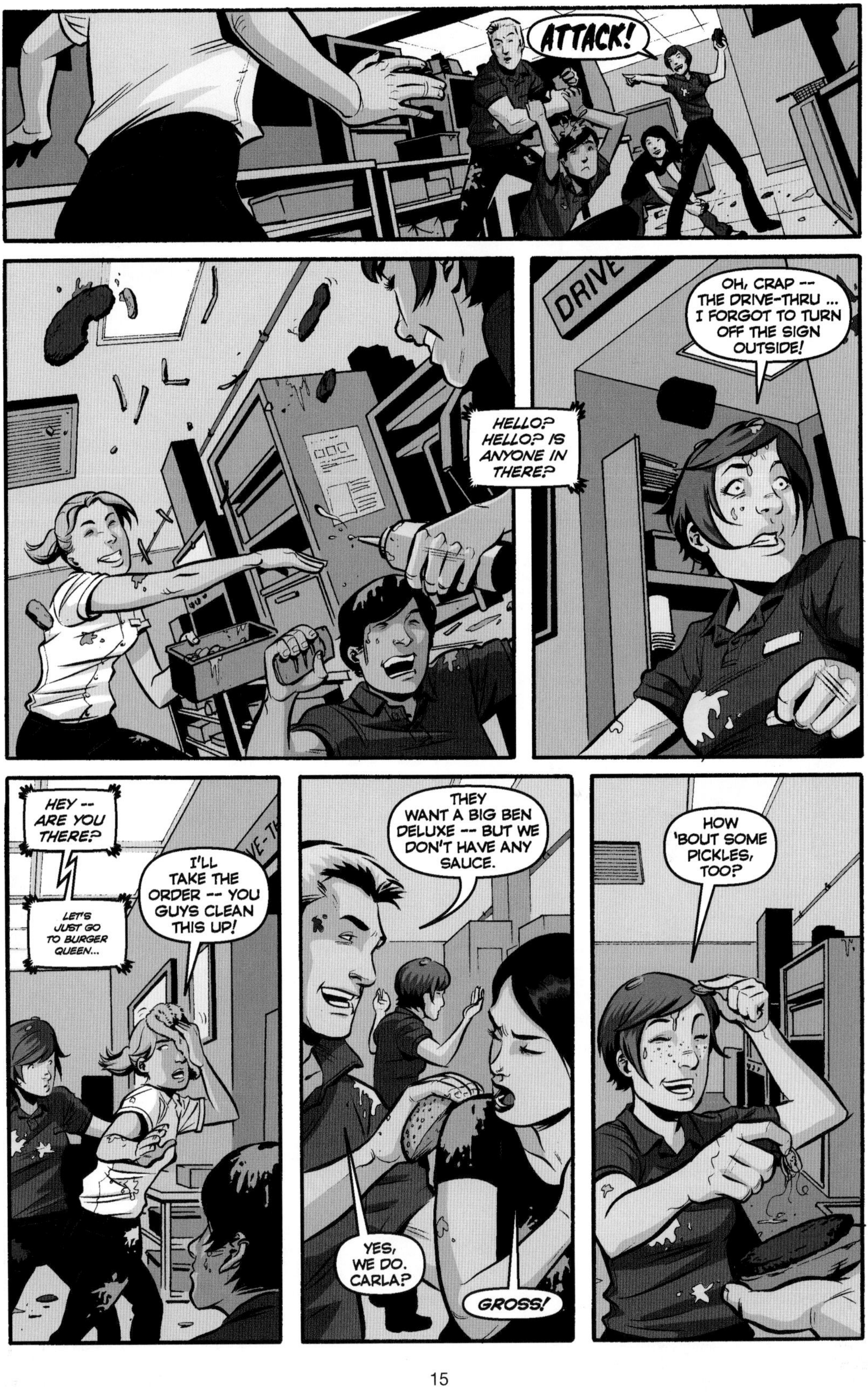
ATTACK!
HELLO? HELLO? IS ANYONE IN THERE?
OH, CRAP -- THE DRIVE-THRU ... I FORGOT TO TURN OFF THE SIGN OUTSIDE!
DRIVE
HEY -- ARE YOU THERE?
LET'S JUST GO TO BURGER QUEEN...
I'LL TAKE THE ORDER -- YOU GUYS CLEAN THIS UP!
THEY WANT A BIG BEN DELUXE -- BUT WE DON'T HAVE ANY SAUCE.
YES, WE DO. CARLA?
GROSS!
HOW 'BOUT SOME PICKLES, TOO?

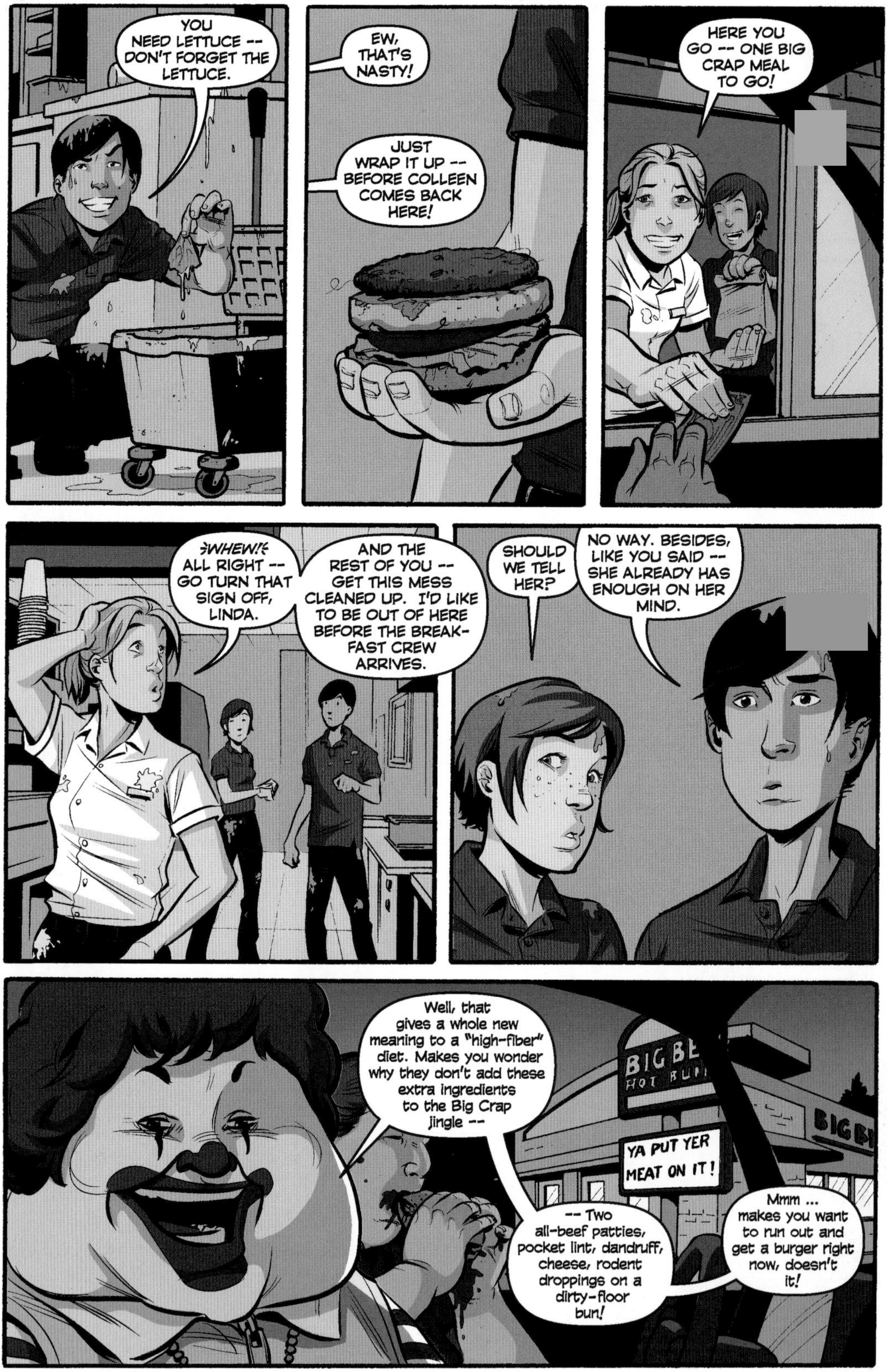
YOU NEED LETTUCE -- DON'T FORGET THE LETTUCE.
EW, THAT'S NASTY!
JUST WRAP IT UP -- BEFORE COLLEEN COMES BACK HERE!
HERE YOU GO -- ONE BIG CRAP MEAL TO GO!
WHEW! ALL RIGHT -- GO TURN THAT SIGN OFF, LINDA.
AND THE REST OF YOU -- GET THIS MESS CLEANED UP. I'D LIKE TO BE OUT OF HERE BEFORE THE BREAK-FAST CREW ARRIVES.
SHOULD WE TELL HER?
NO WAY. BESIDES, LIKE YOU SAID -- SHE ALREADY HAS ENOUGH ON HER MIND.
Well, that gives a whole new meaning to a "high-fiber" diet. Makes you wonder why they don't add these extra ingredients to the Big Crap jingle --
-- Two all-beef patties, pocket lint, dandruff, cheese, rodent droppings on a dirty-floor bun!
Mmm ... makes you want to run out and get a burger right now, doesn't it!
YA PUT YER MEAT ON IT!

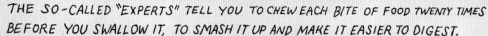

THE SO-CALLED "EXPERTS" TELL YOU TO CHEW EACH BITE OF FOOD TWENTY TIMES BEFORE YOU SWALLOW IT, TO SMASH IT UP AND MAKE IT EASIER TO DIGEST.
WENDELLS
WENDELL'S
THAT'S ALL WELL AND GOOD, BUT SOMETIMES YOU'RE HUNGRY, MAN! SOMETIMES YOU JUST HAVE TO GET IT IN THERE!! SOMETIMES NOT EVERYTHING MAKES IT TO YOUR STOMACH. SOMETIMES YOU HAVE TO TAKE...
THE BIGGEST GULP!
DRAWINGS BY TONY MILLIONAIRE
COLORS BY JIM CAMPBELL
TAKE JOHN, HERE, FOR EXAMPLE...
GULP!! GULP!!
BIGGIE
WENDELL'S
HE'S A HARD-WORKING, EAT-ON-THE-GO KIND OF GUY. WHEN IT COMES TO HIS LUNCH BREAK, HE'S IN, OUT, AND BACK ON THE JOB... NO TIME TO DO ANYTHING ELSE.
YOU WASH THAT BURGER AND FRIES DOWN WITH THAT MUCH SODA AND ICE, AND IT'S GONNA MAKE YOUR THROAT FEEL A LITTLE STRANGE.
BURGERS
HRMPH!
A COLD LITTLE TICKLE, MAYBE?
IT'S NOTHING TO WORRY ABOUT...
HACK!
RIGHT?

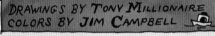

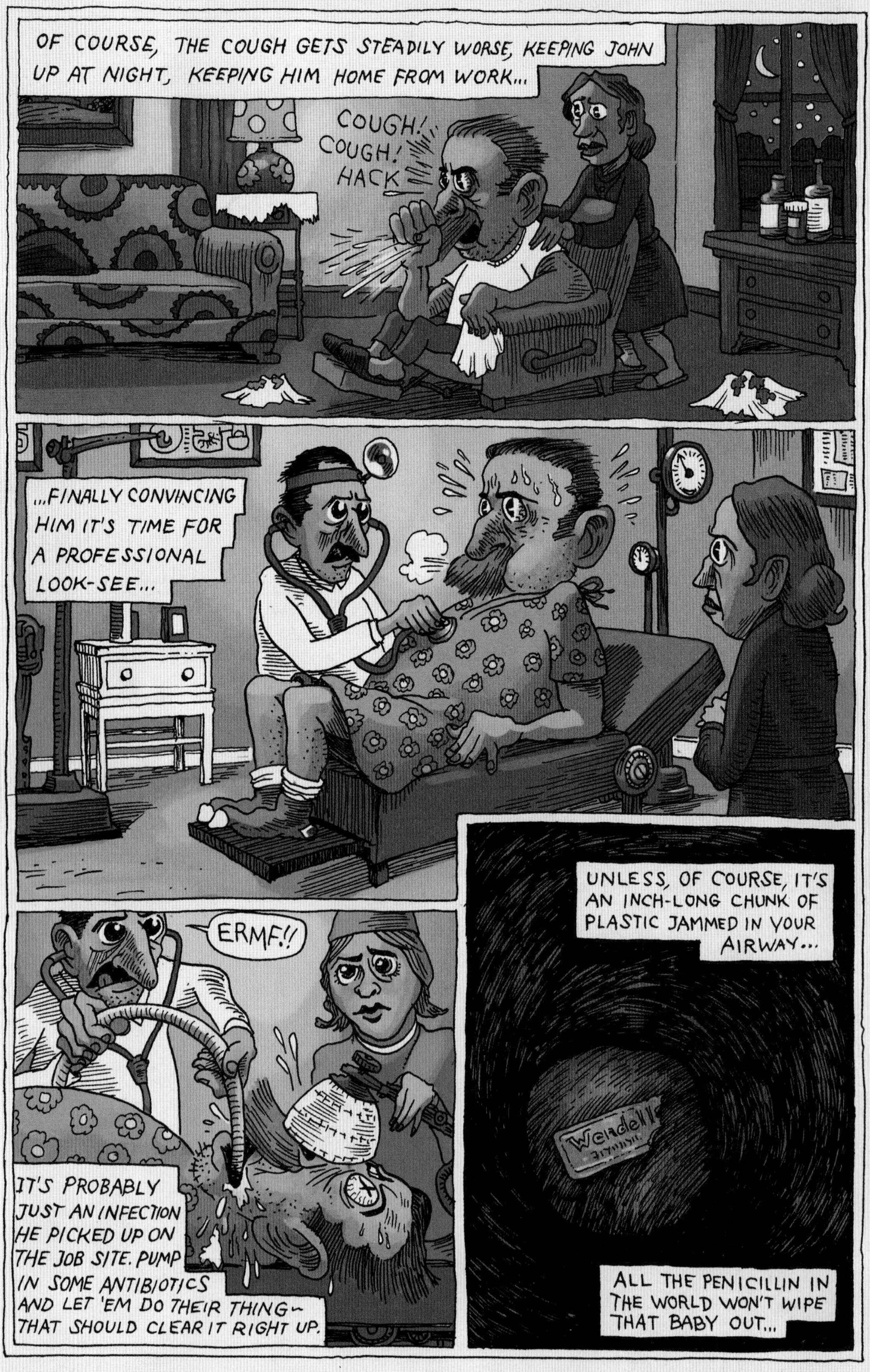
OF COURSE, THE COUGH GETS STEADILY WORSE, KEEPING JOHN UP AT NIGHT, KEEPING HIM HOME FROM WORK...
COUGH! COUGH! HACK
...FINALLY CONVINCING HIM IT'S TIME FOR A PROFESSIONAL LOOK-SEE...
ERMF!!
IT'S PROBABLY JUST AN INFECTION HE PICKED UP ON THE JOB SITE. PUMP IN SOME ANTIBIOTICS AND LET 'EM DO THEIR THING— THAT SHOULD CLEAR IT RIGHT UP.
UNLESS, OF COURSE, IT'S AN INCH-LONG CHUNK OF PLASTIC JAMMED IN YOUR AIRWAY...
Wendell's
ALL THE PENICILLIN IN THE WORLD WON'T WIPE THAT BABY OUT...

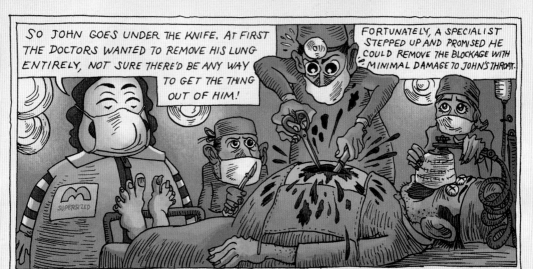

So John goes under the knife. At first the doctors wanted to remove his lung entirely, not sure there'd be any way to get the thing out of him!

Fortunately, a specialist stepped up and promised he could remove the blockage with minimal damage to John's throat.

"A-M-B-U-R-G-E-R" -- gimme an "H" and what do you get?

That's right -- it's the broken end of a Wendell's utensil!

How it got there is anyone's guess!

DOOK! DOOK! DOOK!!

John's health improves almost immediately. Whether that remains so depends on how quickly he returns to his old ways...

... One thing's for sure, though, chewing everything twenty times is one thing -- literally inhaling it is quite another!

END

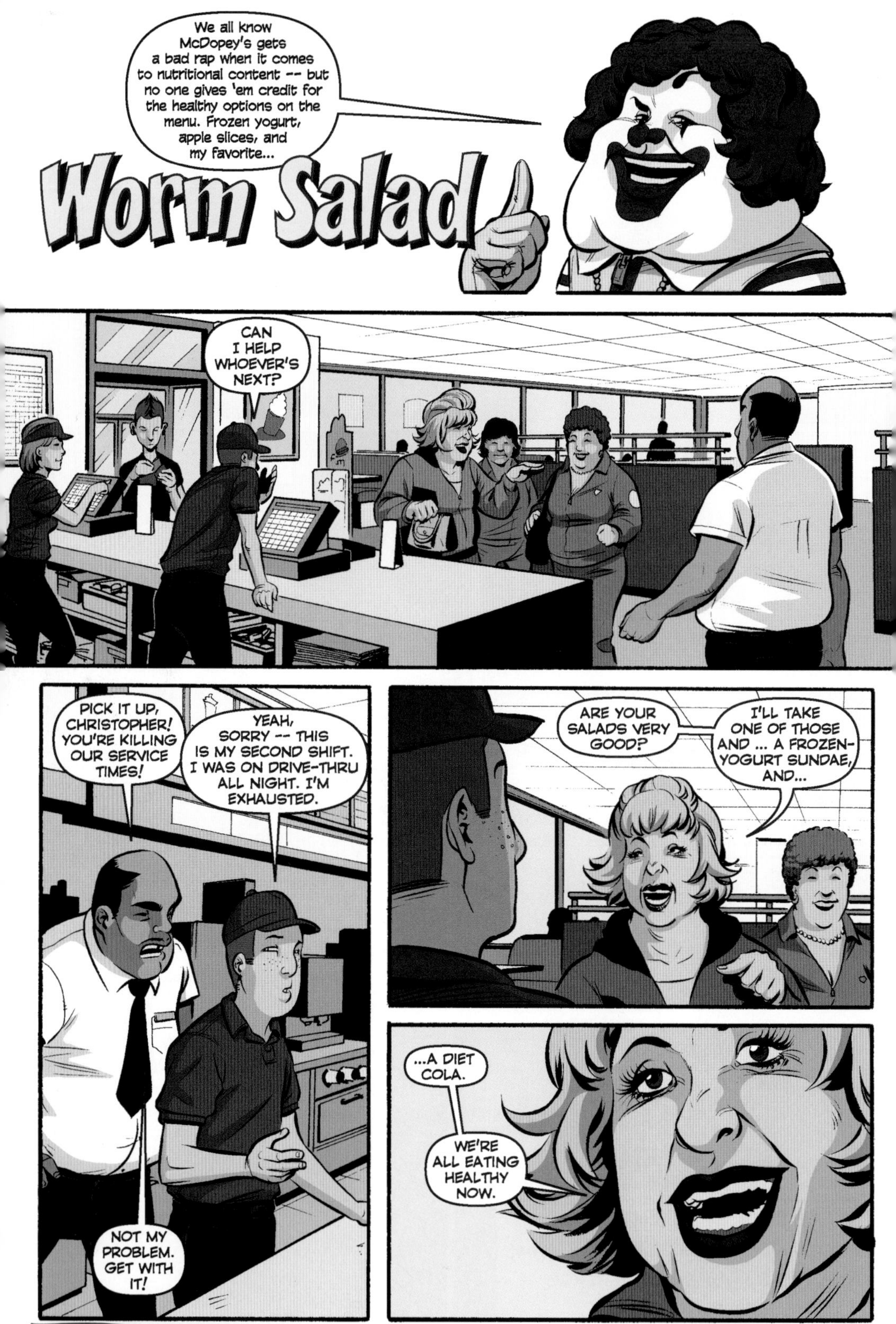

We all know McDopey's gets a bad rap when it comes to nutritional content -- but no one gives 'em credit for the healthy options on the menu. Frozen yogurt, apple slices, and my favorite...
Worm Salad
CAN I HELP WHOEVER'S NEXT?
PICK IT UP, CHRISTOPHER! YOU'RE KILLING OUR SERVICE TIMES!
YEAH, SORRY -- THIS IS MY SECOND SHIFT. I WAS ON DRIVE-THRU ALL NIGHT. I'M EXHAUSTED.
NOT MY PROBLEM. GET WITH IT!
ARE YOUR SALADS VERY GOOD?
I'LL TAKE ONE OF THOSE AND ... A FROZEN-YOGURT SUNDAE, AND...
...A DIET COLA.
WE'RE ALL EATING HEALTHY NOW.

[redacted]

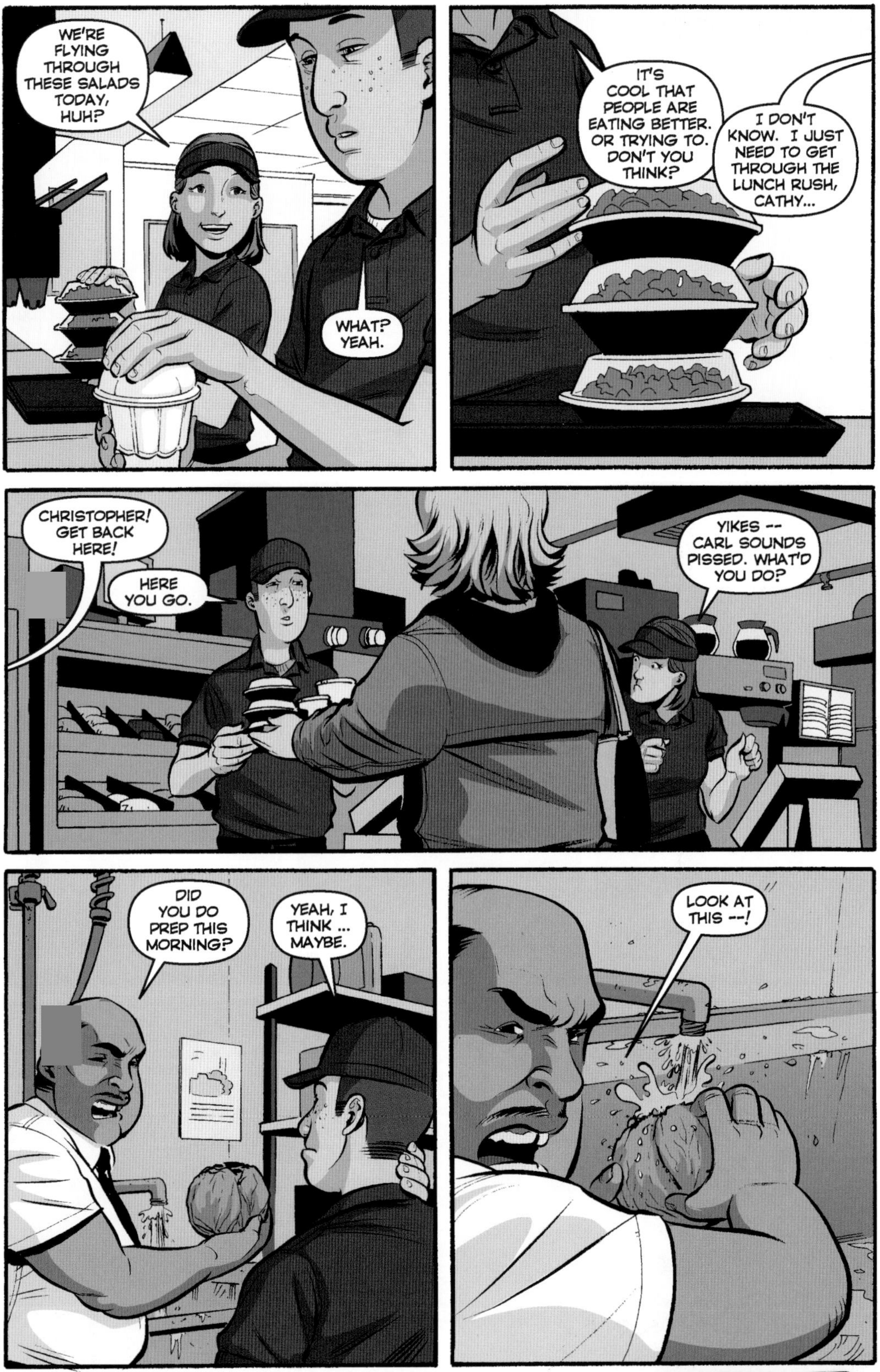
WE'RE FLYING THROUGH THESE SALADS TODAY, HUH?
WHAT? YEAH.
IT'S COOL THAT PEOPLE ARE EATING BETTER. OR TRYING TO. DON'T YOU THINK?
I DON'T KNOW. I JUST NEED TO GET THROUGH THE LUNCH RUSH, CATHY...
CHRISTOPHER! GET BACK HERE!
HERE YOU GO.
YIKES -- CARL SOUNDS PISSED. WHAT'D YOU DO?
DID YOU DO PREP THIS MORNING?
YEAH, I THINK ... MAYBE.
LOOK AT THIS --!

[redacted]

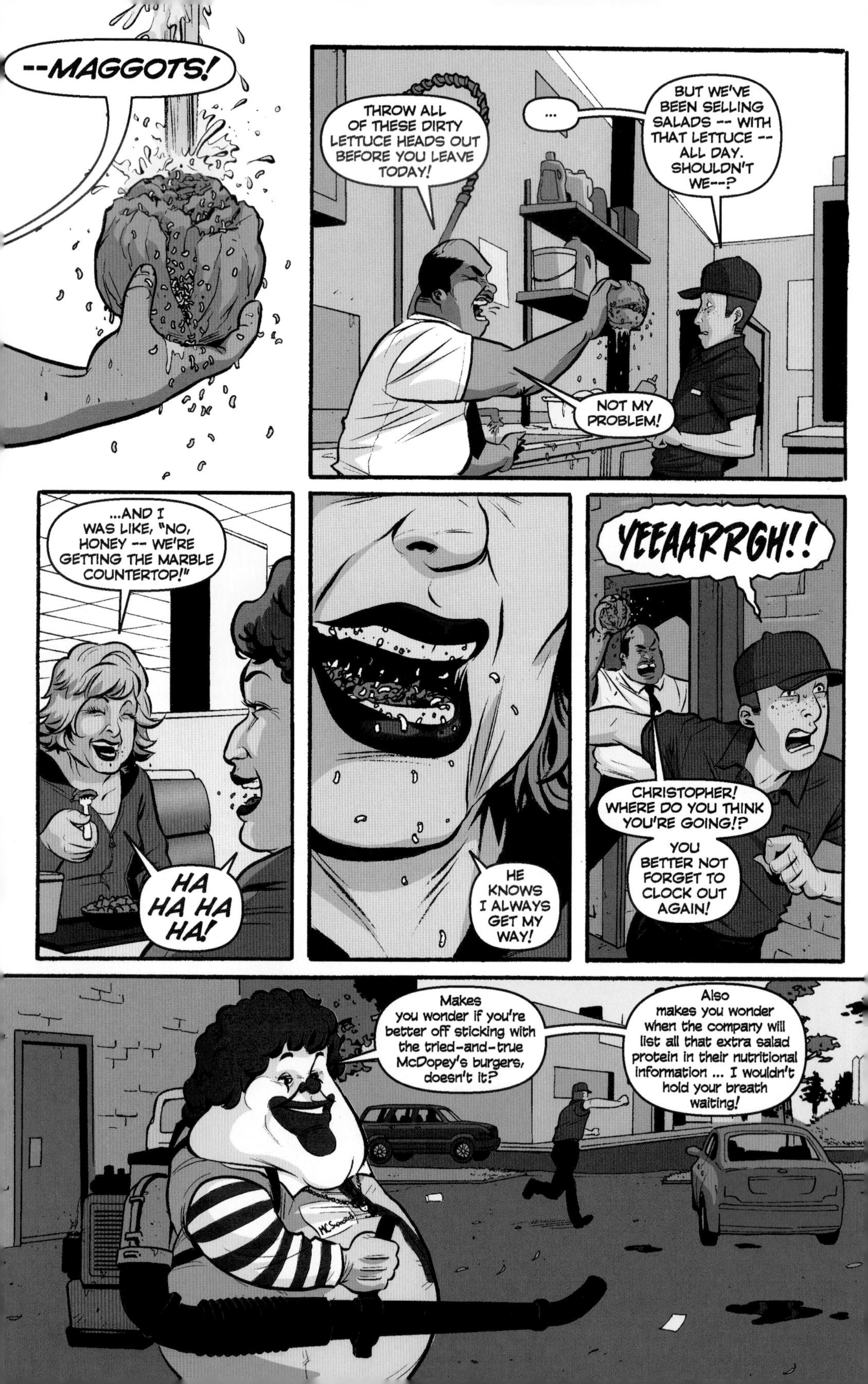
--MAGGOTS!
THROW ALL OF THESE DIRTY LETTUCE HEADS OUT BEFORE YOU LEAVE TODAY!
...
BUT WE'VE BEEN SELLING SALADS -- WITH THAT LETTUCE -- ALL DAY. SHOULDN'T WE--?
NOT MY PROBLEM!
...AND I WAS LIKE, "NO, HONEY -- WE'RE GETTING THE MARBLE COUNTERTOP!"
HA HA HA HA!
HE KNOWS I ALWAYS GET MY WAY!
YEEAARRGH!!
CHRISTOPHER! WHERE DO YOU THINK YOU'RE GOING!?
YOU BETTER NOT FORGET TO CLOCK OUT AGAIN!
Makes you wonder if you're better off sticking with the tried-and-true McDopey's burgers, doesn't it?
Also makes you wonder when the company will list all that extra salad protein in their nutritional information ... I wouldn't hold your breath waiting!

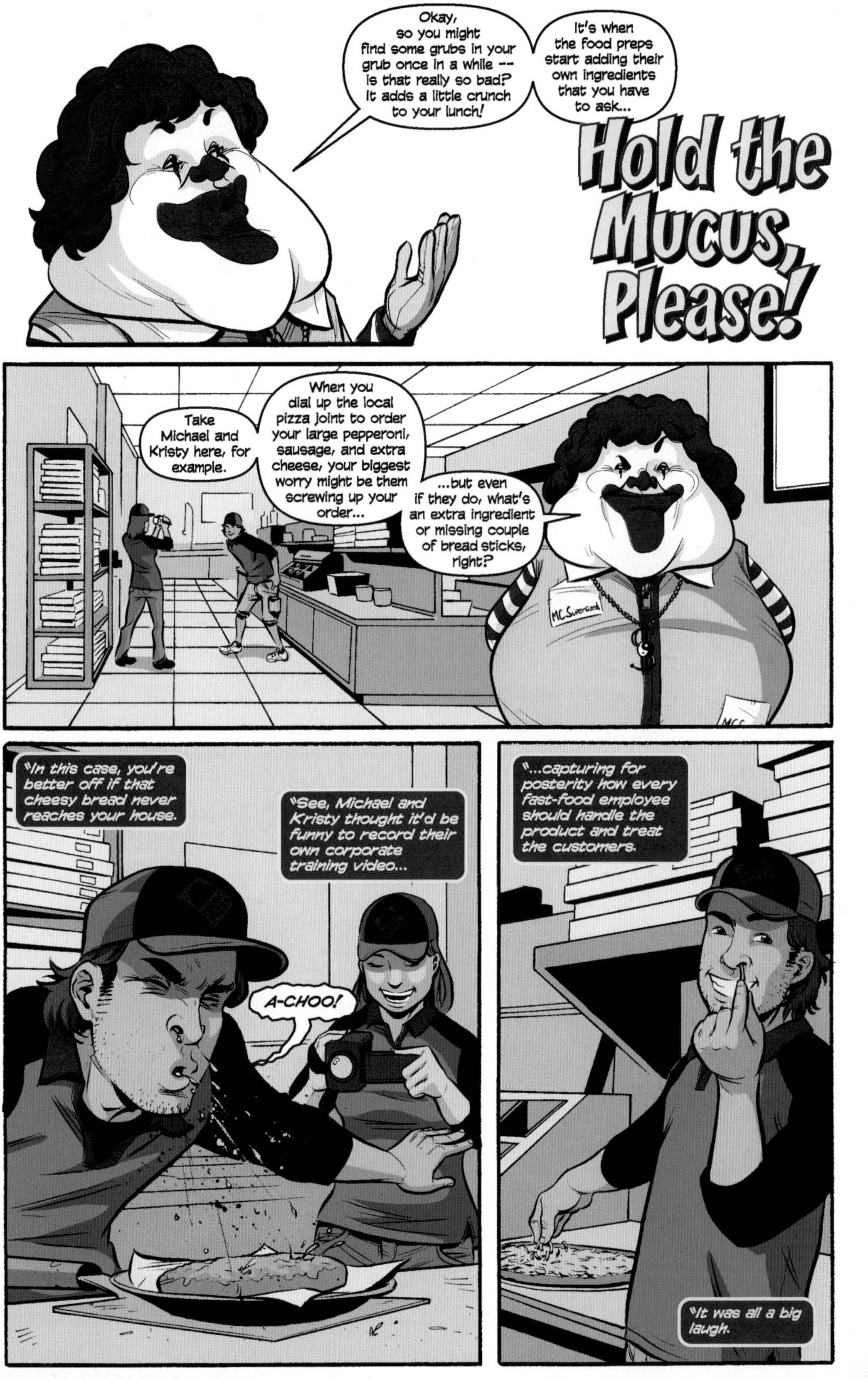
Okay, so you might find some grubs in your grub once in a while -- is that really so bad? It adds a little crunch to your lunch!
It's when the food preps start adding their own ingredients that you have to ask...
Hold the Mucus, Please!
Take Michael and Kristy here, for example.
When you dial up the local pizza joint to order your large pepperoni, sausage, and extra cheese, your biggest worry might be them screwing up your order...
...but even if they do, what's an extra ingredient or missing couple of bread sticks, right?
MC Supersized
"In this case, you're better off if that cheesy bread never reaches your house.
"See, Michael and Kristy thought it'd be funny to record their own corporate training video...
A-CHOO!
"...capturing for posterity how every fast-food employee should handle the product and treat the customers.
"It was all a big laugh.

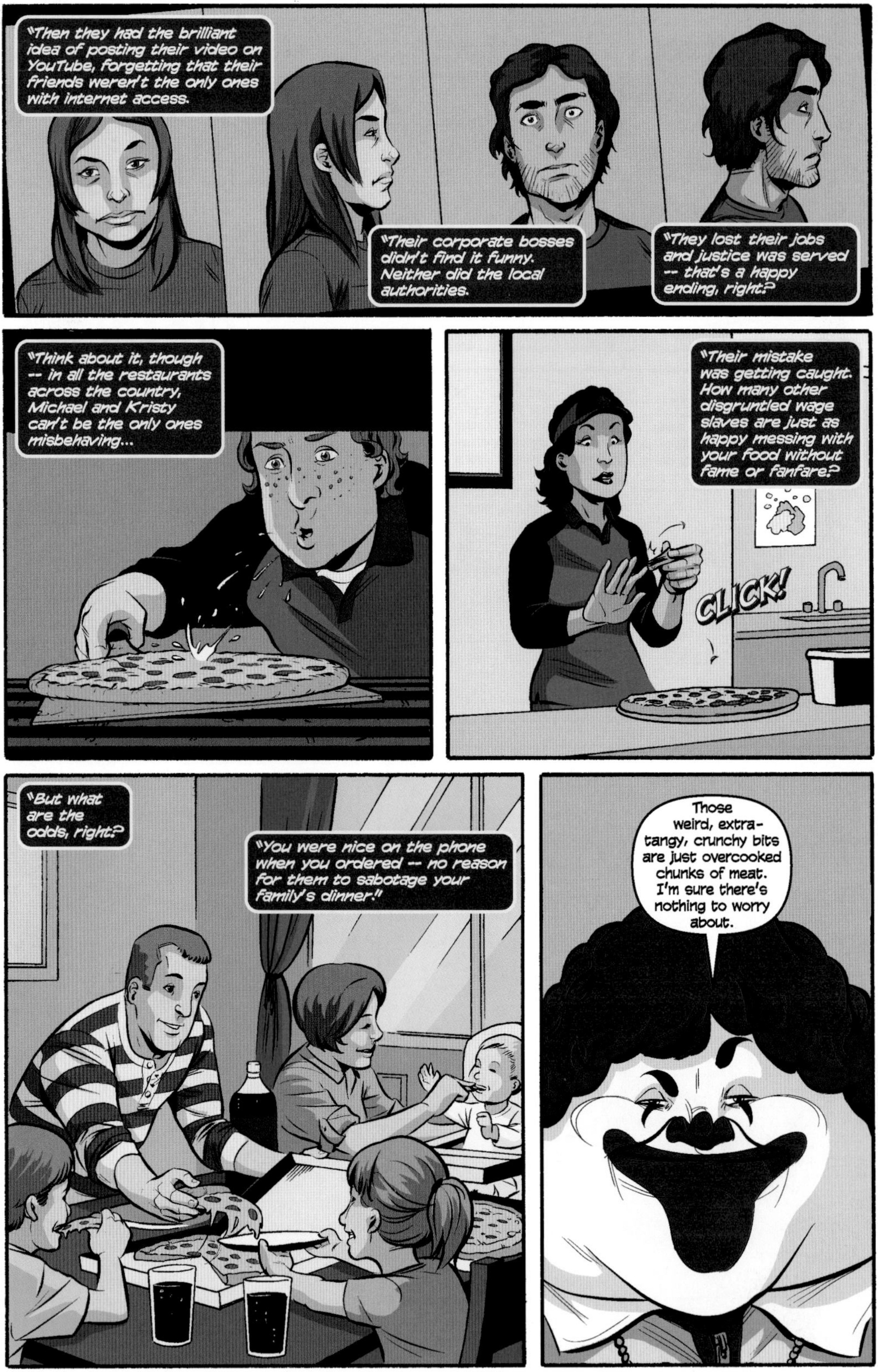

"Then they had the brilliant idea of posting their video on YouTube, forgetting that their friends weren't the only ones with internet access.
"Their corporate bosses didn't find it funny. Neither did the local authorities.
"They lost their jobs and justice was served -- that's a happy ending, right?
"Think about it, though -- in all the restaurants across the country, Michael and Kristy can't be the only ones misbehaving...
"Their mistake was getting caught. How many other disgruntled wage slaves are just as happy messing with your food without fame or fanfare?
CLICK!
"But what are the odds, right?
"You were nice on the phone when you ordered -- no reason for them to sabotage your family's dinner."
Those weird, extra-tangy, crunchy bits are just overcooked chunks of meat. I'm sure there's nothing to worry about.

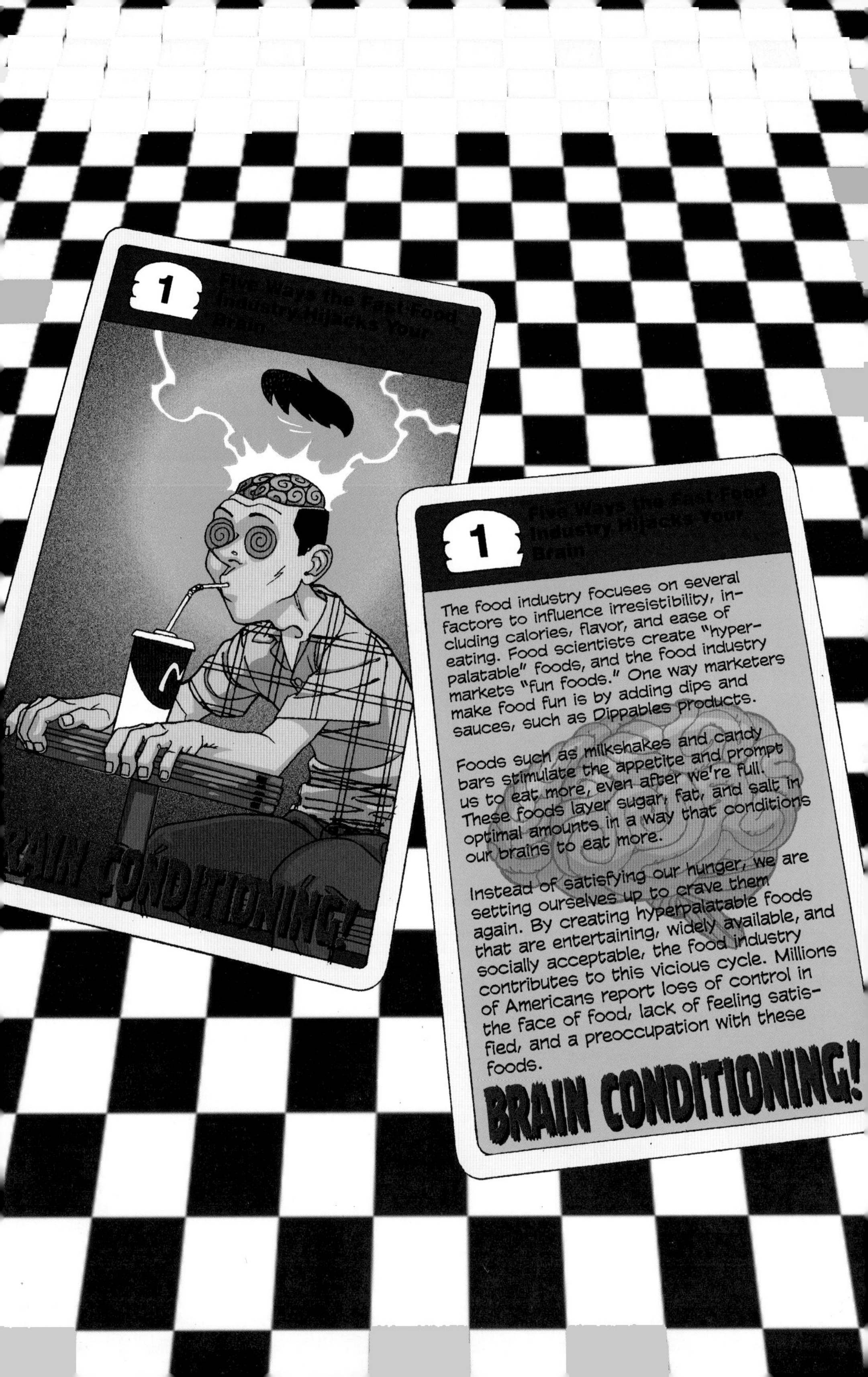
1
Five Ways the Fast-Food Industry Hijacks Your Brain
BRAIN CONDITIONING!
1
Five Ways the Fast-Food Industry Hijacks Your Brain
The food industry focuses on several factors to influence irresistibility, including calories, flavor, and ease of eating. Food scientists create "hyperpalatable" foods, and the food industry markets "fun foods." One way marketers make food fun is by adding dips and sauces, such as Dippables products.
Foods such as milkshakes and candy bars stimulate the appetite and prompt us to eat more, even after we're full. These foods layer sugar, fat, and salt in optimal amounts in a way that conditions our brains to eat more.
Instead of satisfying our hunger, we are setting ourselves up to crave them again. By creating hyperpalatable foods that are entertaining, widely available, and socially acceptable, the food industry contributes to this vicious cycle. Millions of Americans report loss of control in the face of food, lack of feeling satisfied, and a preoccupation with these foods.
BRAIN CONDITIONING!

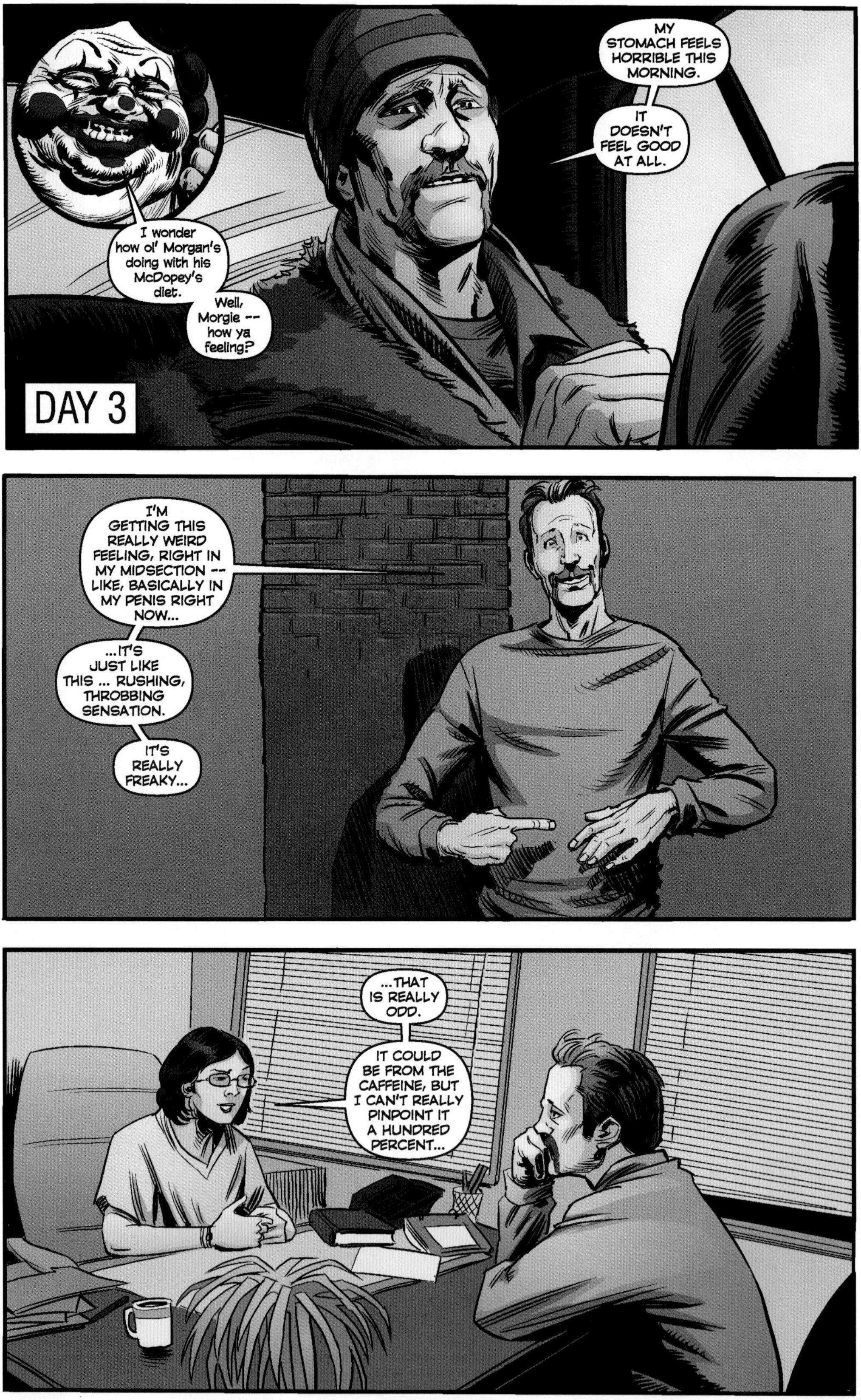
DAY 3
I wonder how ol' Morgan's doing with his McDopey's diet.
Well, Morgie -- how ya feeling?
MY STOMACH FEELS HORRIBLE THIS MORNING.
IT DOESN'T FEEL GOOD AT ALL.
I'M GETTING THIS REALLY WEIRD FEELING, RIGHT IN MY MIDSECTION -- LIKE, BASICALLY IN MY PENIS RIGHT NOW...
...IT'S JUST LIKE THIS ... RUSHING, THROBBING SENSATION.
IT'S REALLY FREAKY...
...THAT IS REALLY ODD.
IT COULD BE FROM THE CAFFEINE, BUT I CAN'T REALLY PINPOINT IT A HUNDRED PERCENT...

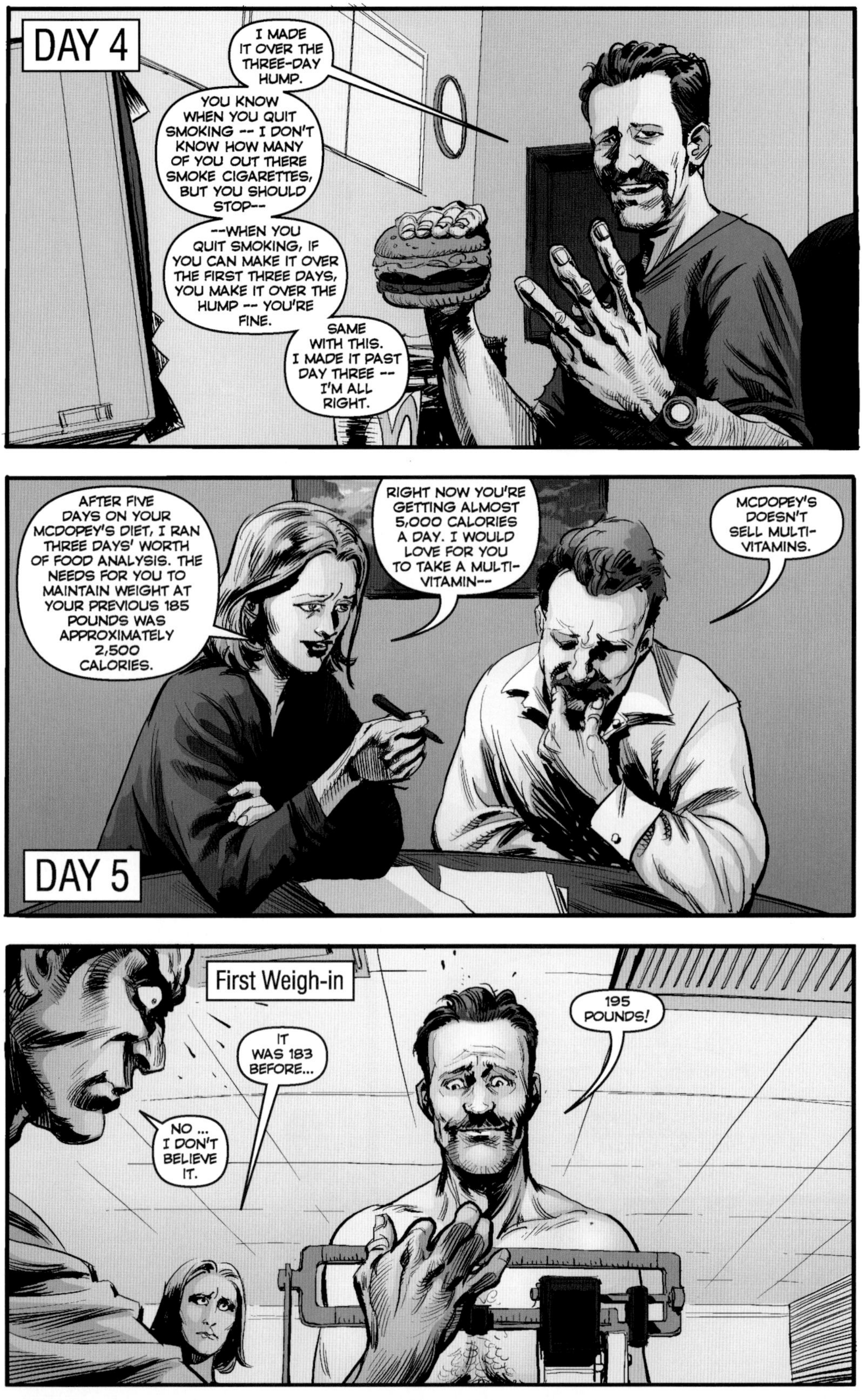
DAY 4
I MADE IT OVER THE THREE-DAY HUMP.
YOU KNOW WHEN YOU QUIT SMOKING -- I DON'T KNOW HOW MANY OF YOU OUT THERE SMOKE CIGARETTES, BUT YOU SHOULD STOP--
--WHEN YOU QUIT SMOKING, IF YOU CAN MAKE IT OVER THE FIRST THREE DAYS, YOU MAKE IT OVER THE HUMP -- YOU'RE FINE.
SAME WITH THIS. I MADE IT PAST DAY THREE -- I'M ALL RIGHT.
AFTER FIVE DAYS ON YOUR MCDOPEY'S DIET, I RAN THREE DAYS' WORTH OF FOOD ANALYSIS. THE NEEDS FOR YOU TO MAINTAIN WEIGHT AT YOUR PREVIOUS 185 POUNDS WAS APPROXIMATELY 2,500 CALORIES.
RIGHT NOW YOU'RE GETTING ALMOST 5,000 CALORIES A DAY. I WOULD LOVE FOR YOU TO TAKE A MULTI-VITAMIN--
MCDOPEY'S DOESN'T SELL MULTI-VITAMINS.
DAY 5
First Weigh-in
195 POUNDS!
IT WAS 183 BEFORE...
NO ... I DON'T BELIEVE IT.

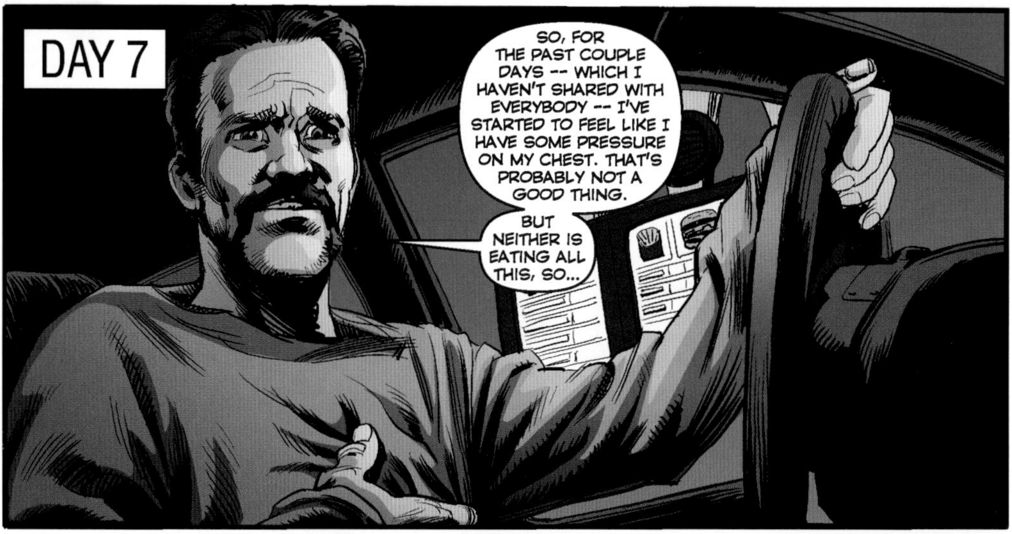
DAY 7
SO, FOR THE PAST COUPLE DAYS -- WHICH I HAVEN'T SHARED WITH EVERYBODY -- I'VE STARTED TO FEEL LIKE I HAVE SOME PRESSURE ON MY CHEST. THAT'S PROBABLY NOT A GOOD THING.
BUT NEITHER IS EATING ALL THIS, SO...

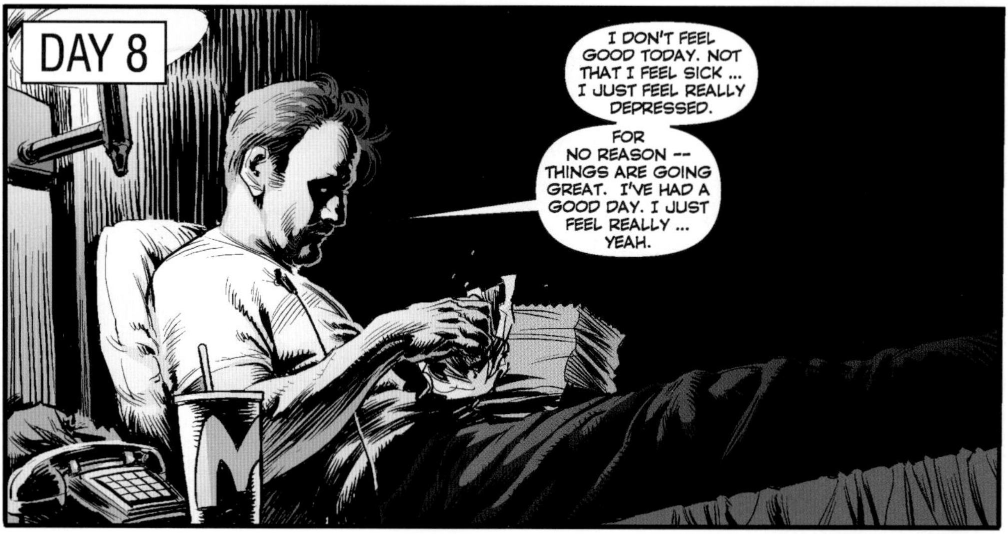
DAY 8
I DON'T FEEL GOOD TODAY. NOT THAT I FEEL SICK ... I JUST FEEL REALLY DEPRESSED.
FOR NO REASON -- THINGS ARE GOING GREAT. I'VE HAD A GOOD DAY. I JUST FEEL REALLY ... YEAH.

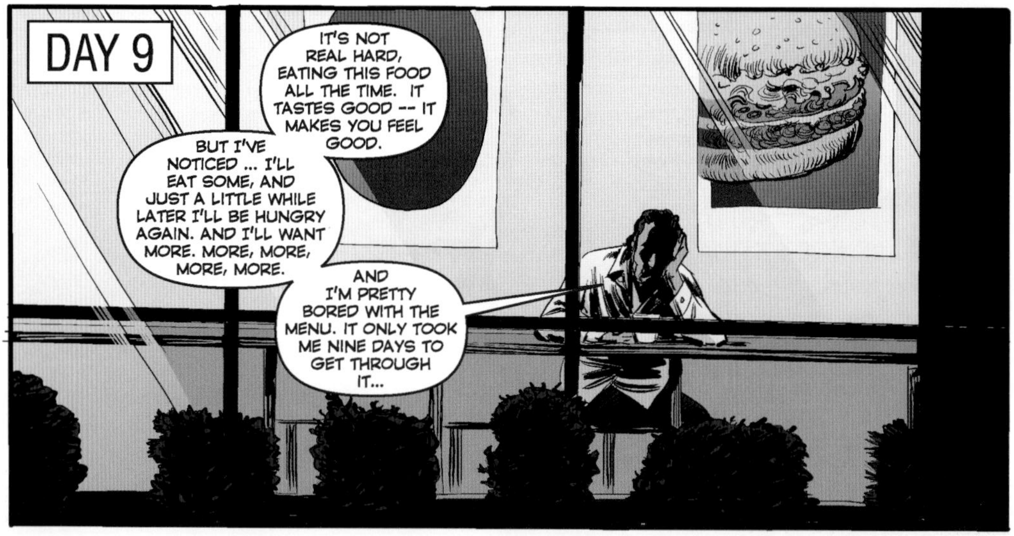
DAY 9
IT'S NOT REAL HARD, EATING THIS FOOD ALL THE TIME. IT TASTES GOOD -- IT MAKES YOU FEEL GOOD.
BUT I'VE NOTICED ... I'LL EAT SOME, AND JUST A LITTLE WHILE LATER I'LL BE HUNGRY AGAIN. AND I'LL WANT MORE. MORE, MORE, MORE, MORE.
AND I'M PRETTY BORED WITH THE MENU. IT ONLY TOOK ME NINE DAYS TO GET THROUGH IT...

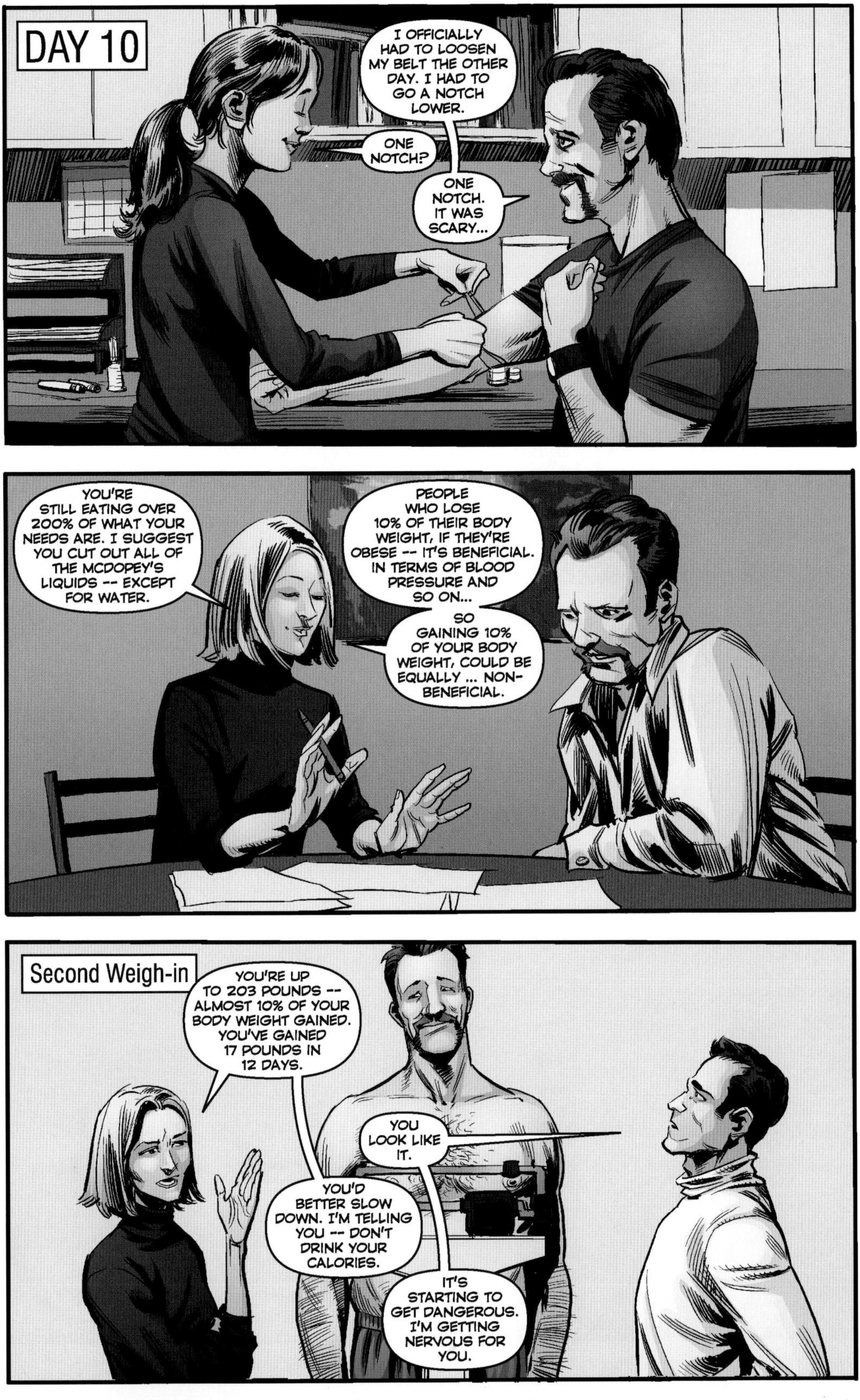
DAY 10
I OFFICIALLY HAD TO LOOSEN MY BELT THE OTHER DAY. I HAD TO GO A NOTCH LOWER.
ONE NOTCH?
ONE NOTCH. IT WAS SCARY...
YOU'RE STILL EATING OVER 200% OF WHAT YOUR NEEDS ARE. I SUGGEST YOU CUT OUT ALL OF THE MCDOPEY'S LIQUIDS -- EXCEPT FOR WATER.
PEOPLE WHO LOSE 10% OF THEIR BODY WEIGHT, IF THEY'RE OBESE -- IT'S BENEFICIAL. IN TERMS OF BLOOD PRESSURE AND SO ON...
SO GAINING 10% OF YOUR BODY WEIGHT, COULD BE EQUALLY ... NON-BENEFICIAL.
Second Weigh-in
YOU'RE UP TO 203 POUNDS -- ALMOST 10% OF YOUR BODY WEIGHT GAINED. YOU'VE GAINED 17 POUNDS IN 12 DAYS.
YOU LOOK LIKE IT.
YOU'D BETTER SLOW DOWN. I'M TELLING YOU -- DON'T DRINK YOUR CALORIES.
IT'S STARTING TO GET DANGEROUS. I'M GETTING NERVOUS FOR YOU.

The Smoking Fry

Day One

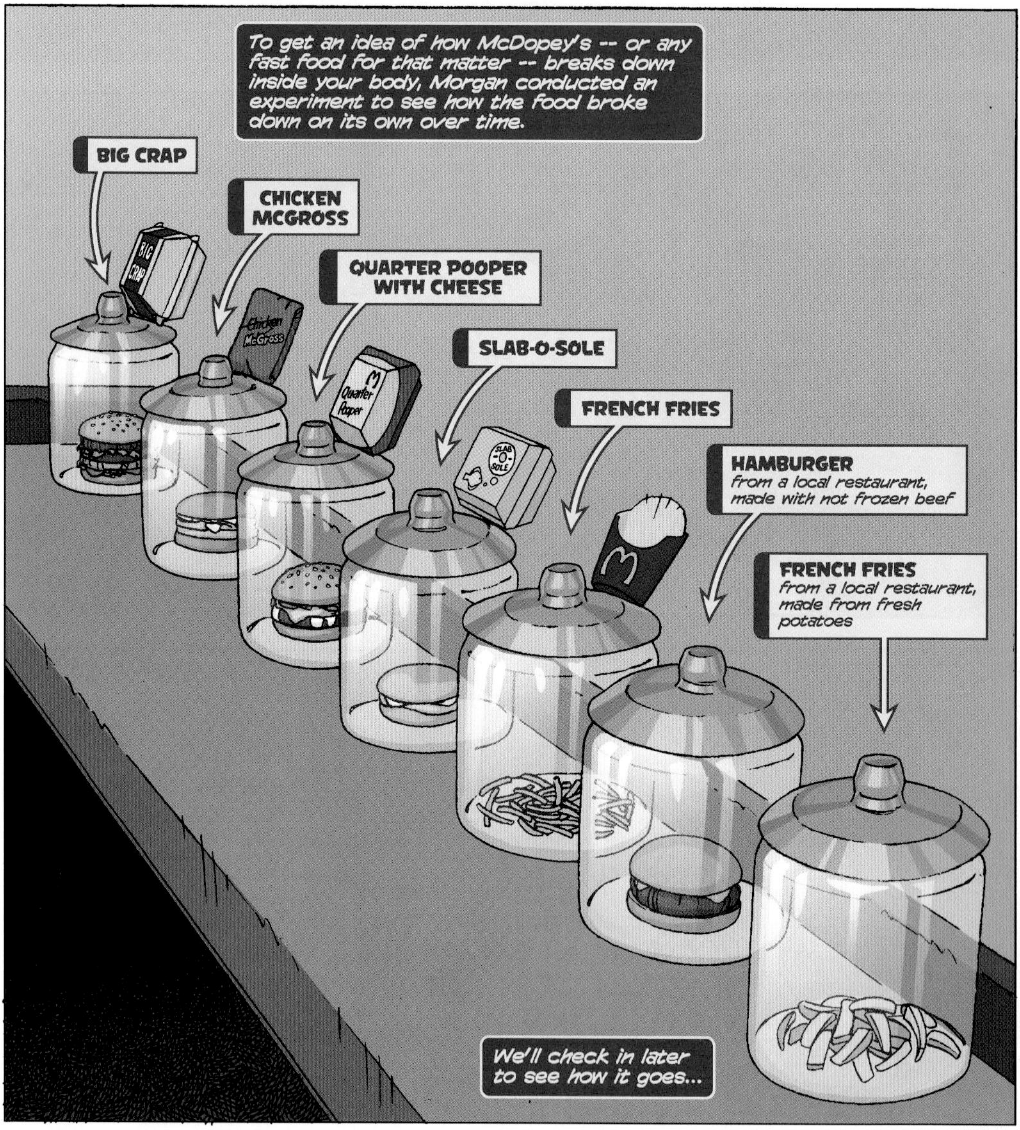

To get an idea of how McDopey's -- or any fast food for that matter -- breaks down inside your body, Morgan conducted an experiment to see how the food broke down on its own over time.
BIG CRAP
CHICKEN MCGROSS
QUARTER POOPER WITH CHEESE
SLAB-O-SOLE
FRENCH FRIES
HAMBURGER
from a local restaurant, made with not frozen beef
FRENCH FRIES
from a local restaurant, made from fresh potatoes
We'll check in later to see how it goes...

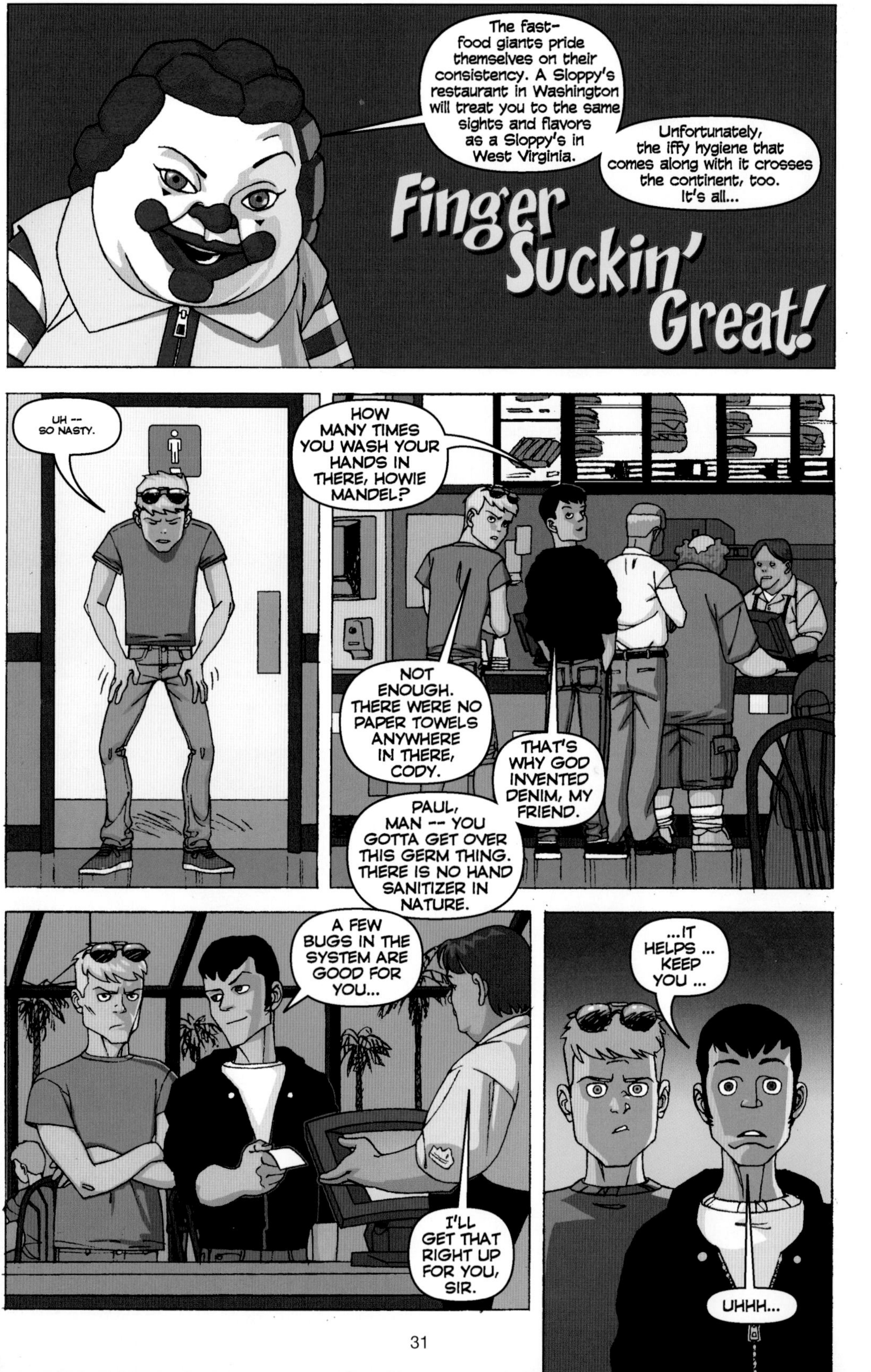

The fast-food giants pride themselves on their consistency. A Sloppy's restaurant in Washington will treat you to the same sights and flavors as a Sloppy's in West Virginia.
Unfortunately, the iffy hygiene that comes along with it crosses the continent, too. It's all...
Finger Suckin' Great!
UH -- SO NASTY.
HOW MANY TIMES YOU WASH YOUR HANDS IN THERE, HOWIE MANDEL?
NOT ENOUGH. THERE WERE NO PAPER TOWELS ANYWHERE IN THERE, CODY.
THAT'S WHY GOD INVENTED DENIM, MY FRIEND.
PAUL, MAN -- YOU GOTTA GET OVER THIS GERM THING. THERE IS NO HAND SANITIZER IN NATURE.
A FEW BUGS IN THE SYSTEM ARE GOOD FOR YOU...
I'LL GET THAT RIGHT UP FOR YOU, SIR.
...IT HELPS ... KEEP YOU ...
UHHH...

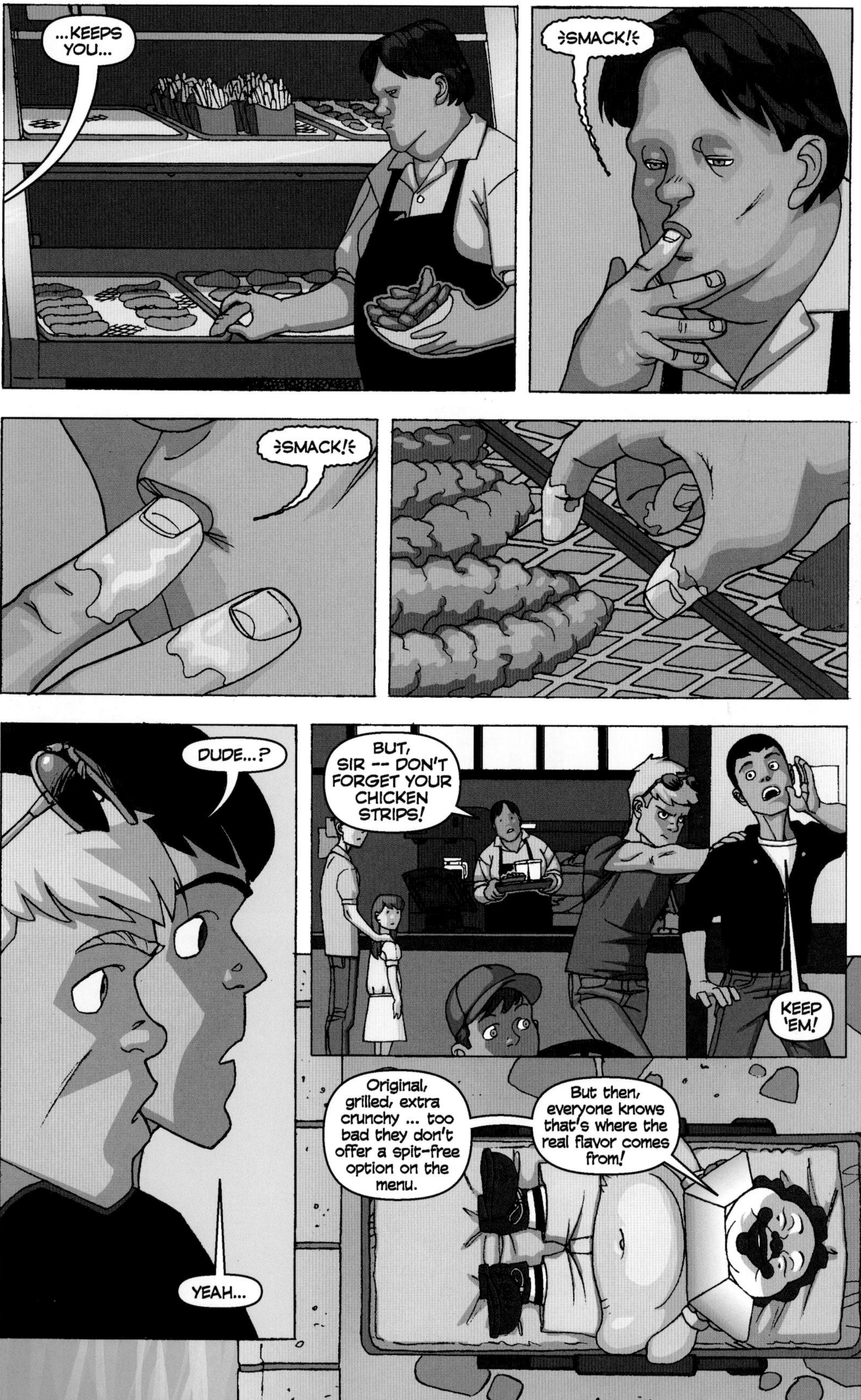
...KEEPS YOU...
SMACK!
SMACK!
DUDE...?
YEAH...
BUT, SIR -- DON'T FORGET YOUR CHICKEN STRIPS!
KEEP 'EM!
Original, grilled, extra crunchy ... too bad they don't offer a spit-free option on the menu.
But then, everyone knows that's where the real flavor comes from!

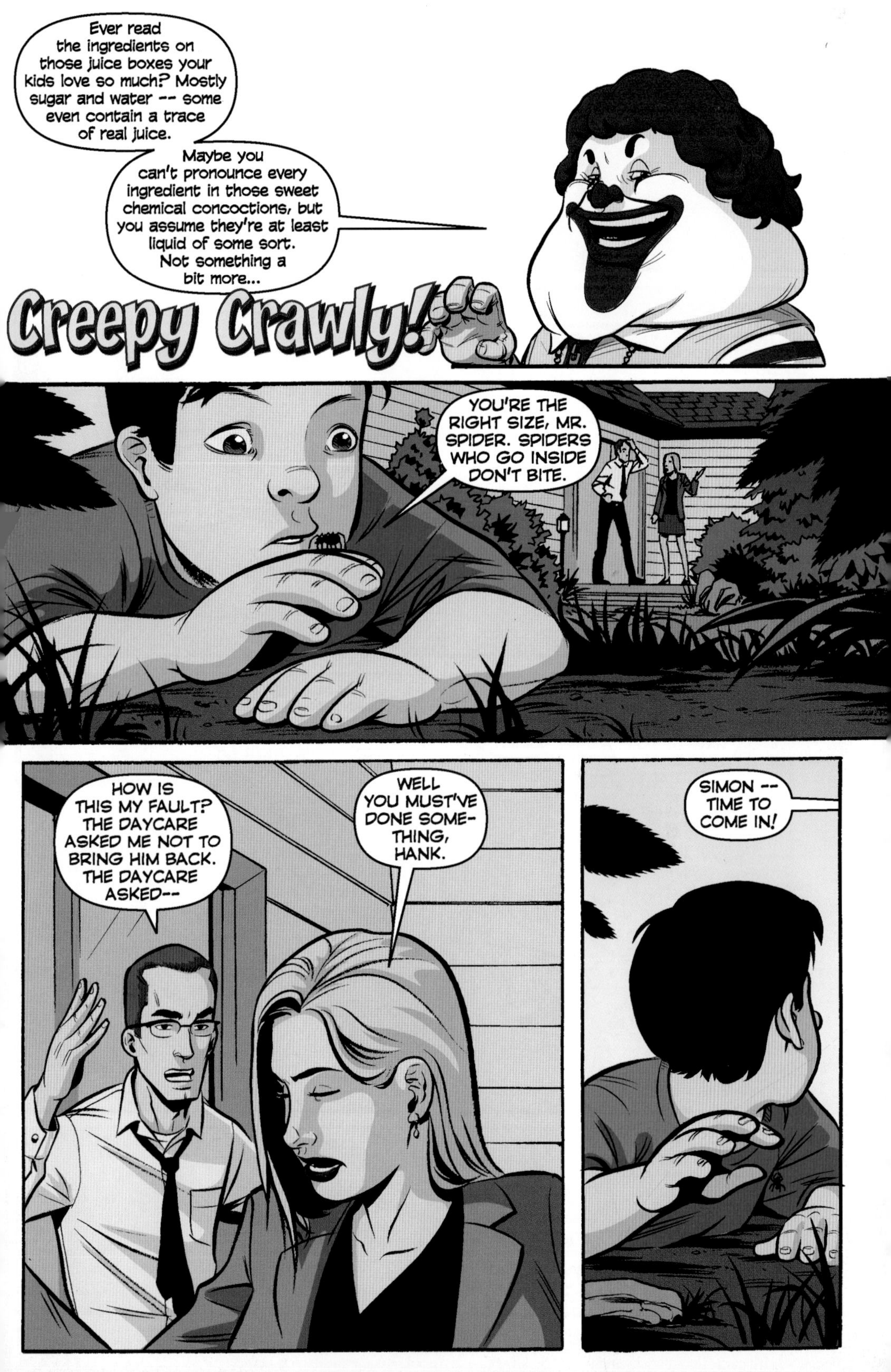
Ever read the ingredients on those juice boxes your kids love so much? Mostly sugar and water -- some even contain a trace of real juice.
Maybe you can't pronounce every ingredient in those sweet chemical concoctions, but you assume they're at least liquid of some sort. Not something a bit more...
Creepy Crawly!
YOU'RE THE RIGHT SIZE, MR. SPIDER. SPIDERS WHO GO INSIDE DON'T BITE.
HOW IS THIS MY FAULT? THE DAYCARE ASKED ME NOT TO BRING HIM BACK. THE DAYCARE ASKED--
WELL YOU MUST'VE DONE SOME-THING, HANK.
SIMON -- TIME TO COME IN!

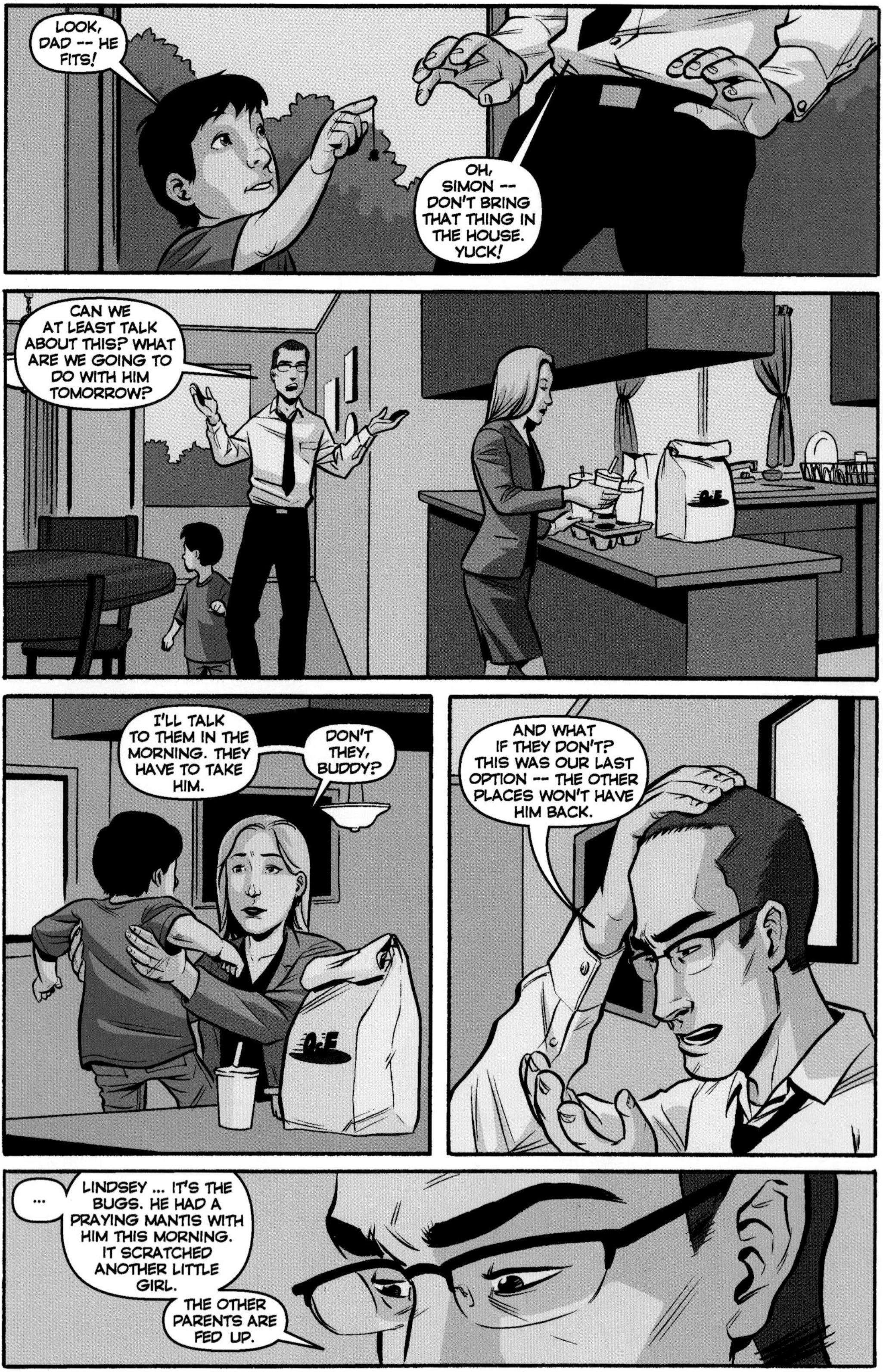
LOOK, DAD -- HE FITS!
OH, SIMON -- DON'T BRING THAT THING IN THE HOUSE. YUCK!
CAN WE AT LEAST TALK ABOUT THIS? WHAT ARE WE GOING TO DO WITH HIM TOMORROW?
I'LL TALK TO THEM IN THE MORNING. THEY HAVE TO TAKE HIM.
DON'T THEY, BUDDY?
AND WHAT IF THEY DON'T? THIS WAS OUR LAST OPTION -- THE OTHER PLACES WON'T HAVE HIM BACK.
...
LINDSEY ... IT'S THE BUGS. HE HAD A PRAYING MANTIS WITH HIM THIS MORNING. IT SCRATCHED ANOTHER LITTLE GIRL.
THE OTHER PARENTS ARE FED UP.

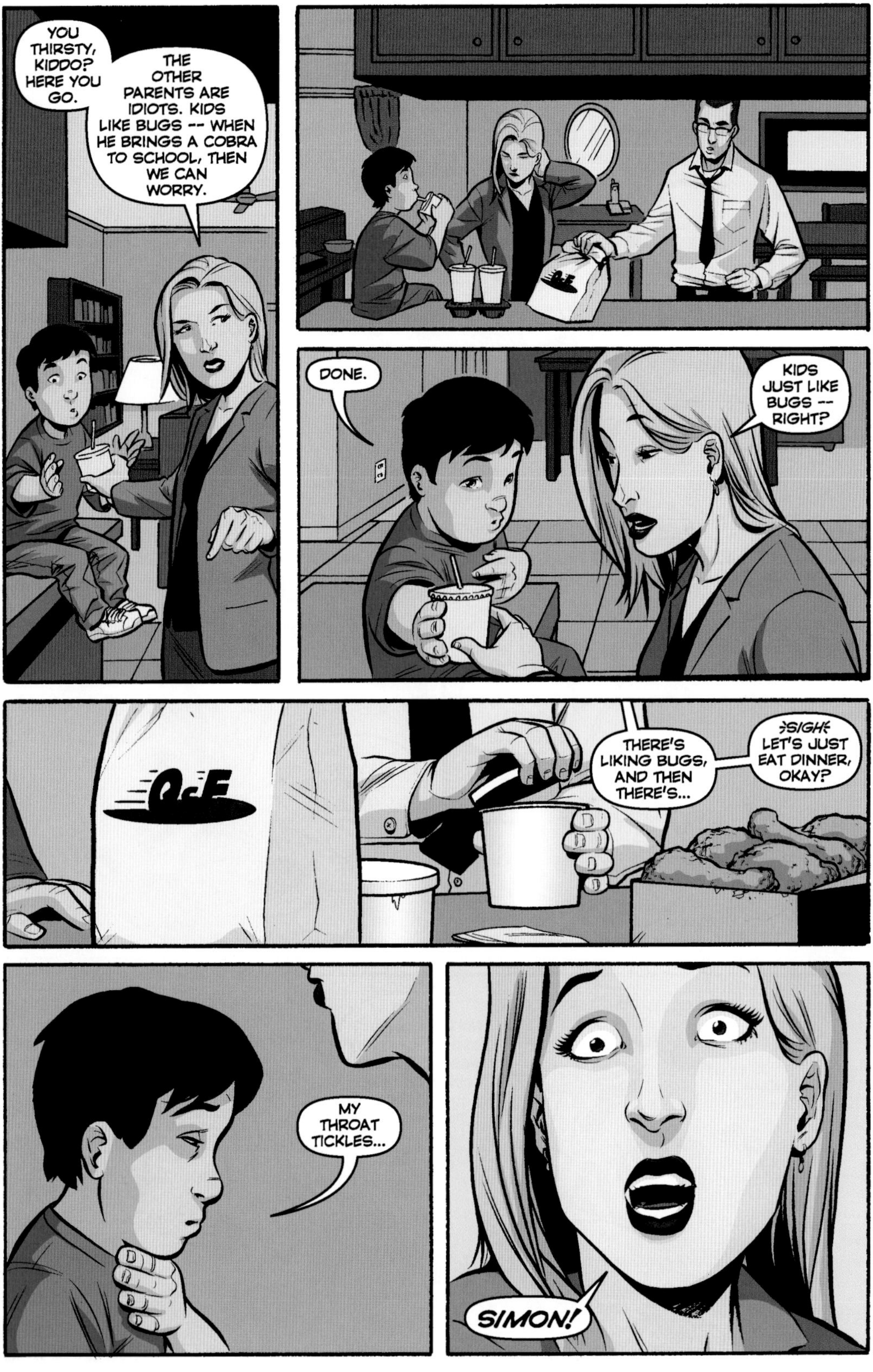
YOU THIRSTY, KIDDO? HERE YOU GO.
THE OTHER PARENTS ARE IDIOTS. KIDS LIKE BUGS -- WHEN HE BRINGS A COBRA TO SCHOOL, THEN WE CAN WORRY.
DONE.
KIDS JUST LIKE BUGS -- RIGHT?
THERE'S LIKING BUGS, AND THEN THERE'S...
SIGH LET'S JUST EAT DINNER, OKAY?
MY THROAT TICKLES...
SIMON!

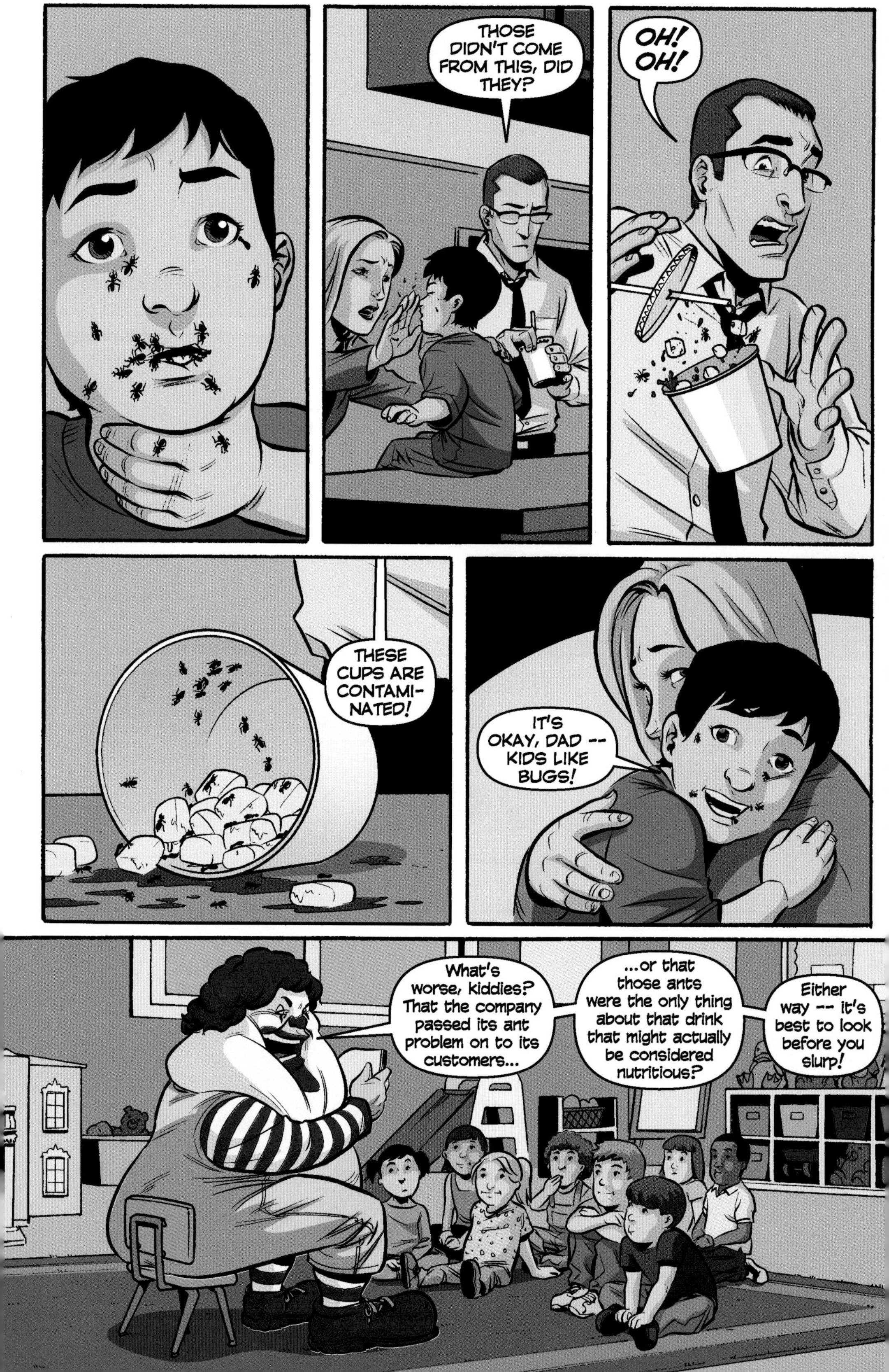
THOSE DIDN'T COME FROM THIS, DID THEY?
OH! OH!
THESE CUPS ARE CONTAMI-NATED!
IT'S OKAY, DAD -- KIDS LIKE BUGS!
What's worse, kiddies? That the company passed its ant problem on to its customers...
...or that those ants were the only thing about that drink that might actually be considered nutritious?
Either way -- it's best to look before you slurp!

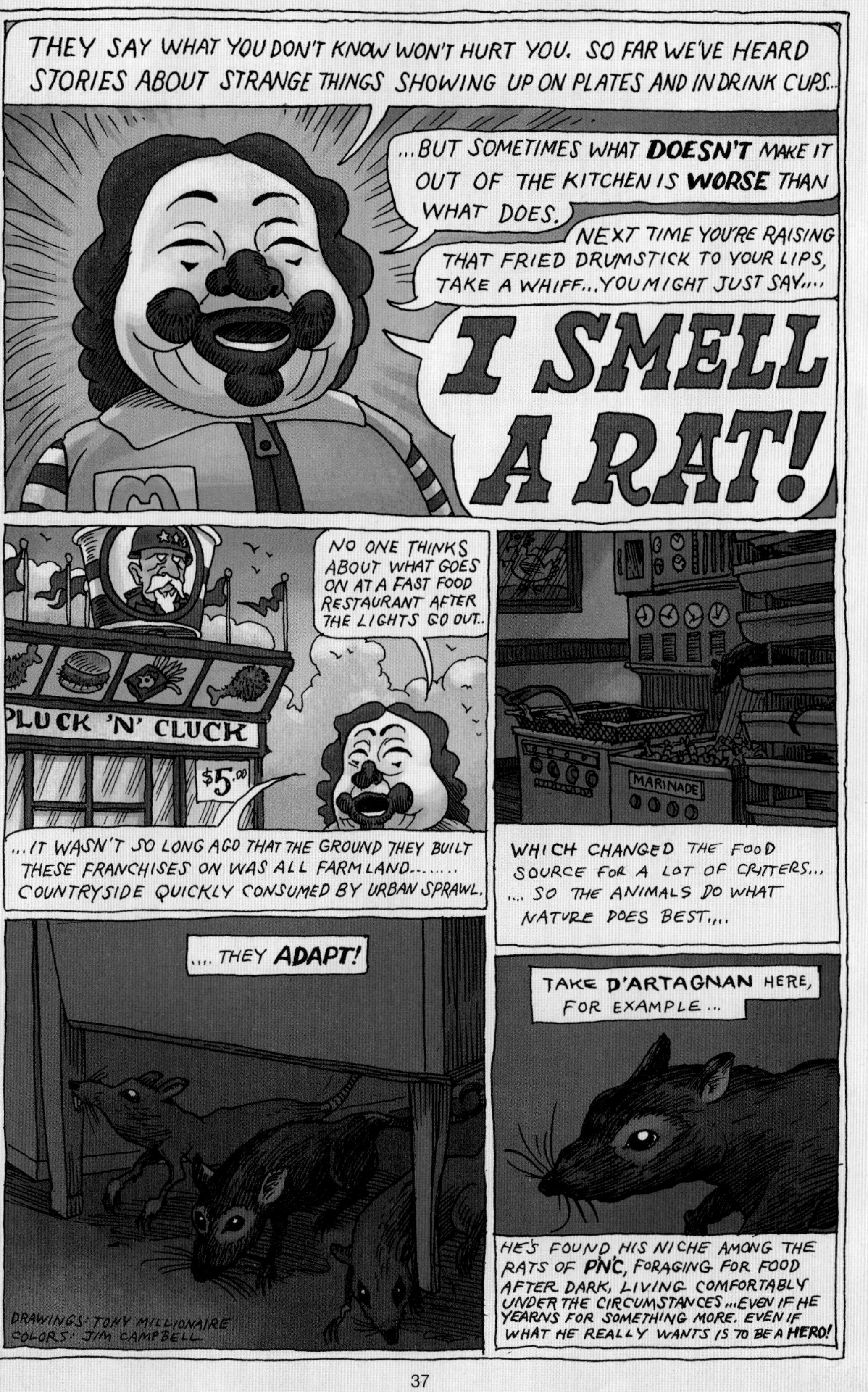
THEY SAY WHAT YOU DON'T KNOW WON'T HURT YOU. SO FAR WE'VE HEARD STORIES ABOUT STRANGE THINGS SHOWING UP ON PLATES AND IN DRINK CUPS...
...BUT SOMETIMES WHAT DOESN'T MAKE IT OUT OF THE KITCHEN IS WORSE THAN WHAT DOES.
NEXT TIME YOU'RE RAISING THAT FRIED DRUMSTICK TO YOUR LIPS, TAKE A WHIFF... YOU MIGHT JUST SAY...
I SMELL A RAT!
NO ONE THINKS ABOUT WHAT GOES ON AT A FAST FOOD RESTAURANT AFTER THE LIGHTS GO OUT..
PLUCK 'N' CLUCK
$5.00
...IT WASN'T SO LONG AGO THAT THE GROUND THEY BUILT THESE FRANCHISES ON WAS ALL FARMLAND....... COUNTRYSIDE QUICKLY CONSUMED BY URBAN SPRAWL.
MARINADE
WHICH CHANGED THE FOOD SOURCE FOR A LOT OF CRITTERS... ... SO THE ANIMALS DO WHAT NATURE DOES BEST...
.... THEY ADAPT!
TAKE D'ARTAGNAN HERE, FOR EXAMPLE...
HE'S FOUND HIS NICHE AMONG THE RATS OF PNC, FORAGING FOR FOOD AFTER DARK, LIVING COMFORTABLY UNDER THE CIRCUMSTANCES... EVEN IF HE YEARNS FOR SOMETHING MORE. EVEN IF WHAT HE REALLY WANTS IS TO BE A HERO!
DRAWINGS: TONY MILLIONAIRE
COLORS: JIM CAMPBELL

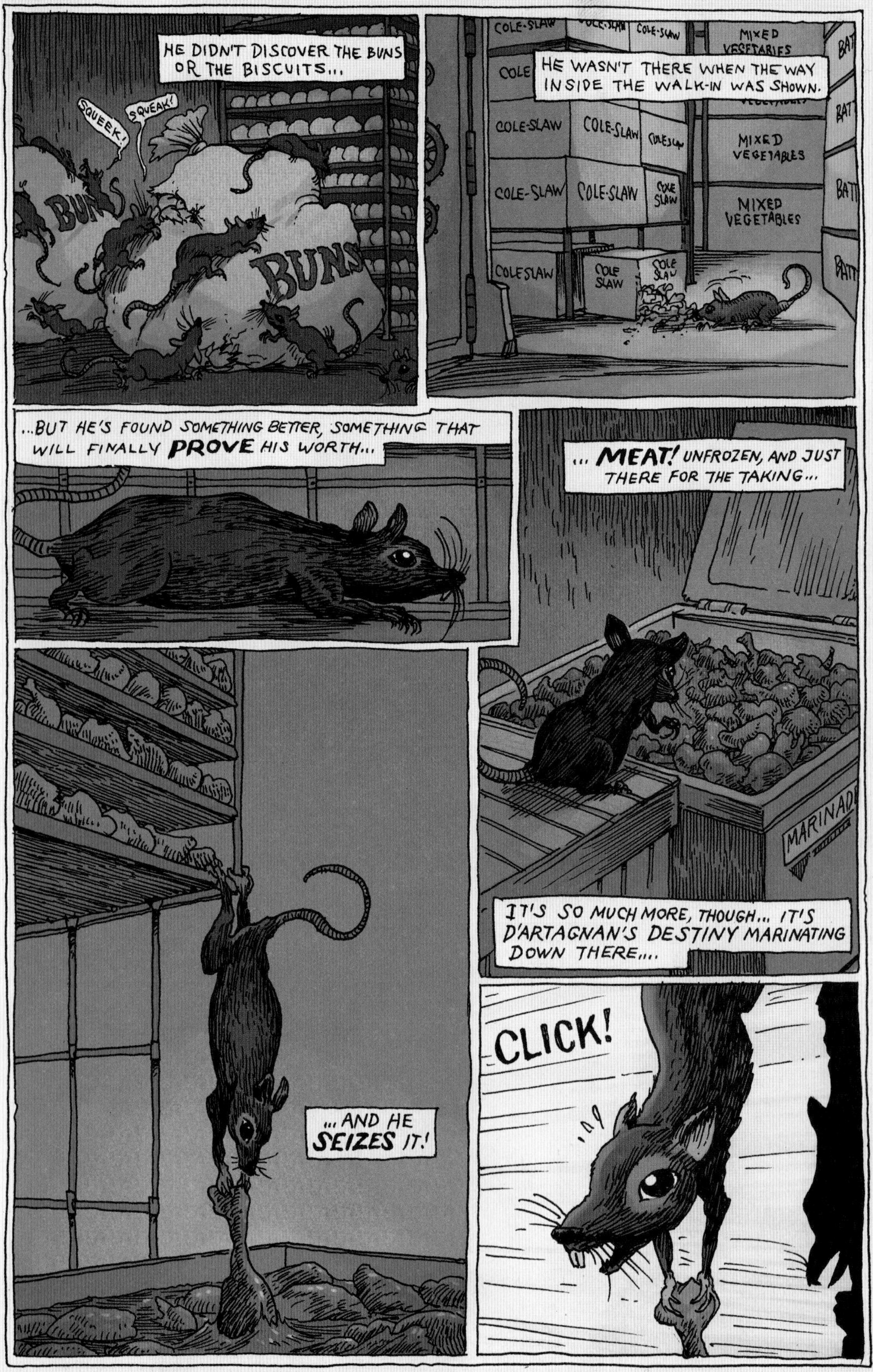
HE DIDN'T DISCOVER THE BUNS OR THE BISCUITS...
SQUEEK!
SQUEAK!
BUNS
BUNS
COLE-SLAW
MIXED VEGETABLES
HE WASN'T THERE WHEN THE WAY INSIDE THE WALK-IN WAS SHOWN.
...BUT HE'S FOUND SOMETHING BETTER, SOMETHING THAT WILL FINALLY PROVE HIS WORTH...
... MEAT! UNFROZEN, AND JUST THERE FOR THE TAKING...
MARINADE
IT'S SO MUCH MORE, THOUGH... IT'S D'ARTAGNAN'S DESTINY MARINATING DOWN THERE....
...AND HE SEIZES IT!
CLICK!

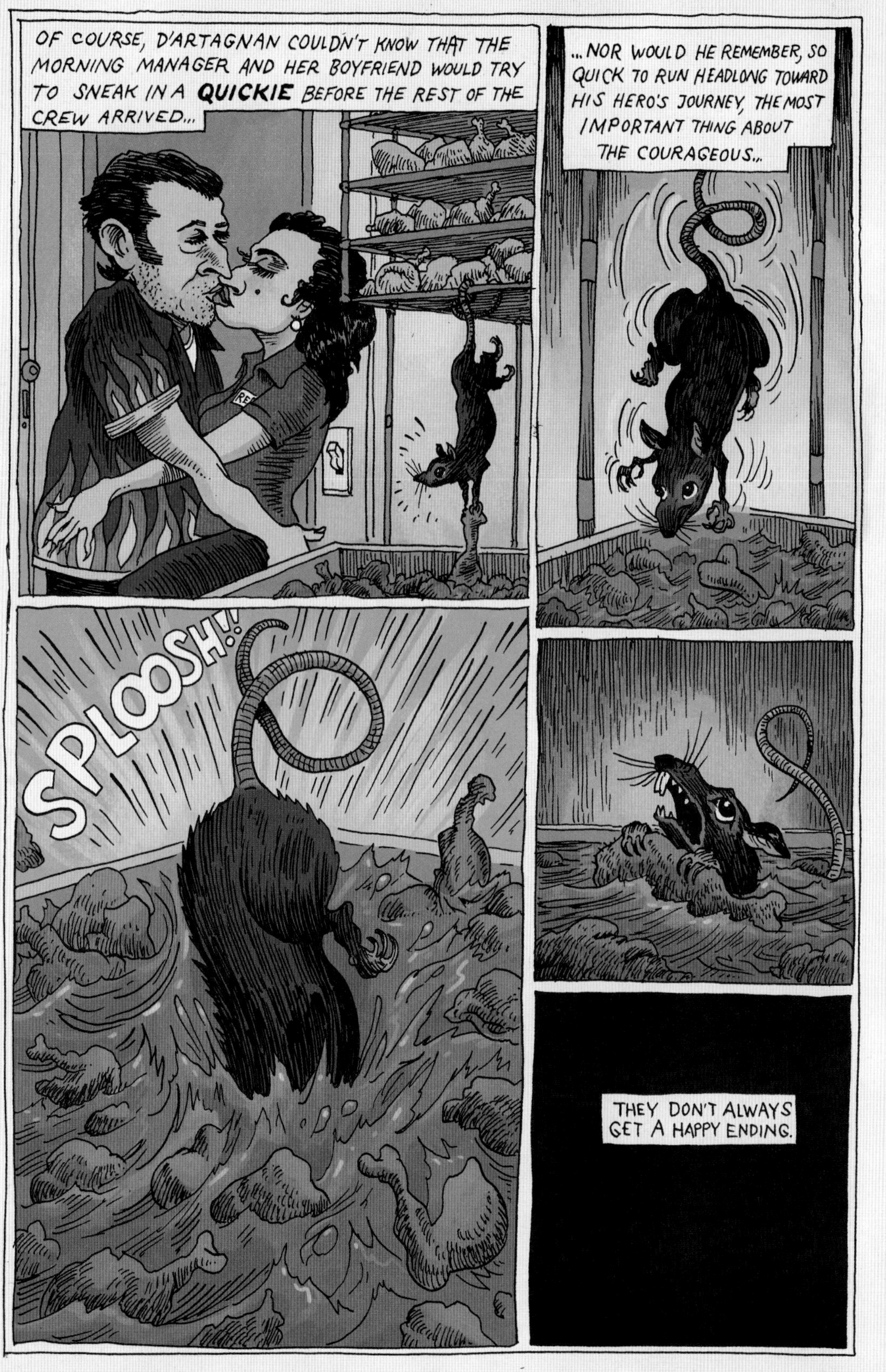
OF COURSE, D'ARTAGNAN COULDN'T KNOW THAT THE MORNING MANAGER AND HER BOYFRIEND WOULD TRY TO SNEAK IN A **QUICKIE** BEFORE THE REST OF THE CREW ARRIVED...
...NOR WOULD HE REMEMBER, SO QUICK TO RUN HEADLONG TOWARD HIS HERO'S JOURNEY, THE MOST IMPORTANT THING ABOUT THE COURAGEOUS...
SPLOOSH!!
THEY DON'T ALWAYS GET A HAPPY ENDING.

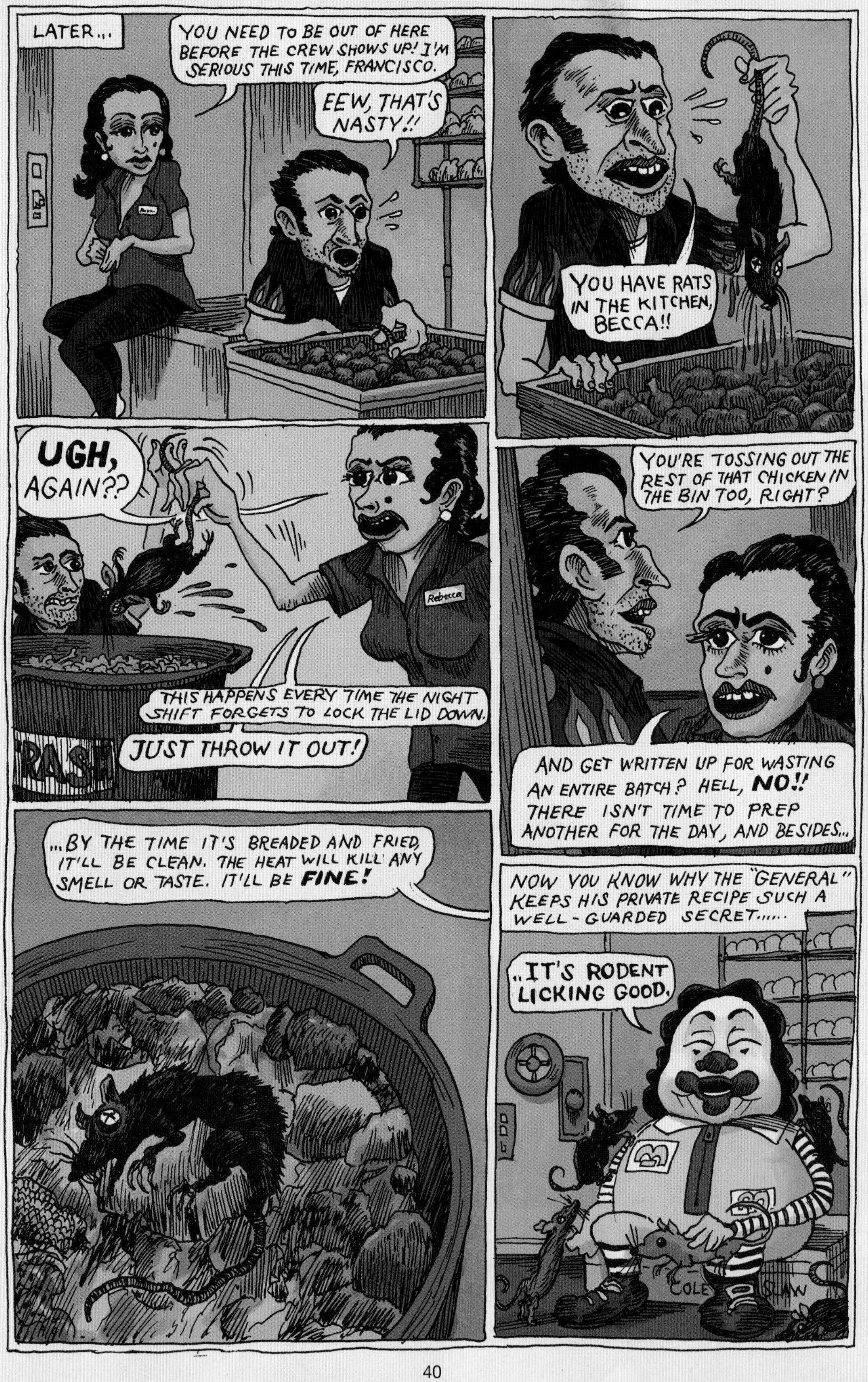
LATER...
YOU NEED TO BE OUT OF HERE BEFORE THE CREW SHOWS UP! I'M SERIOUS THIS TIME, FRANCISCO.
EEW, THAT'S NASTY!!
YOU HAVE RATS IN THE KITCHEN, BECCA!!
UGH, AGAIN??
THIS HAPPENS EVERY TIME THE NIGHT SHIFT FORGETS TO LOCK THE LID DOWN.
JUST THROW IT OUT!
Rebecca
TRASH
YOU'RE TOSSING OUT THE REST OF THAT CHICKEN IN THE BIN TOO, RIGHT?
AND GET WRITTEN UP FOR WASTING AN ENTIRE BATCH? HELL, NO!! THERE ISN'T TIME TO PREP ANOTHER FOR THE DAY, AND BESIDES...
...BY THE TIME IT'S BREADED AND FRIED, IT'LL BE CLEAN. THE HEAT WILL KILL ANY SMELL OR TASTE. IT'LL BE FINE!
NOW YOU KNOW WHY THE "GENERAL" KEEPS HIS PRIVATE RECIPE SUCH A WELL-GUARDED SECRET......
..IT'S RODENT LICKING GOOD.
COLE SLAW

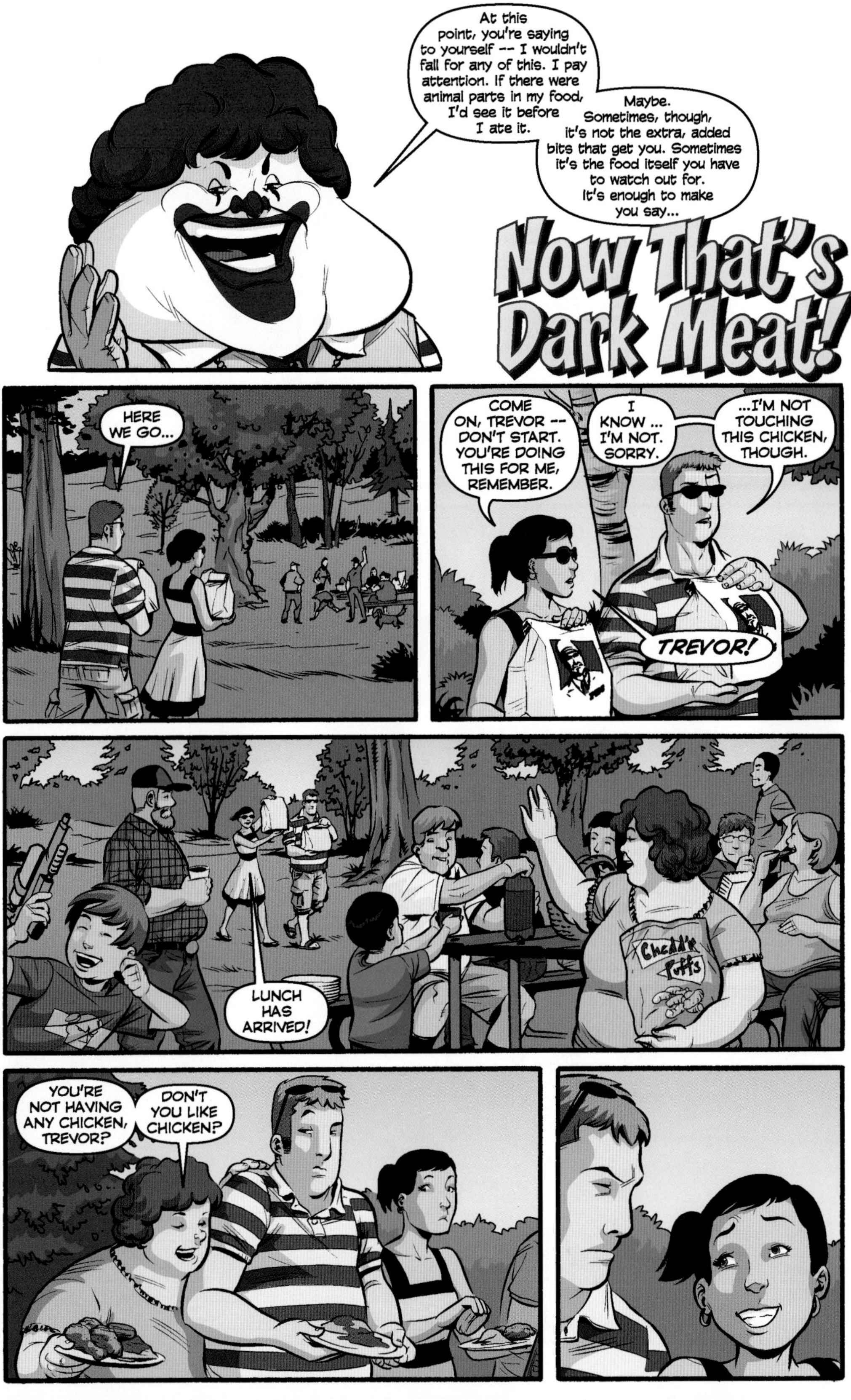

At this point, you're saying to yourself -- I wouldn't fall for any of this. I pay attention. If there were animal parts in my food, I'd see it before I ate it.
Maybe. Sometimes, though, it's not the extra, added bits that get you. Sometimes it's the food itself you have to watch out for. It's enough to make you say...
Now That's Dark Meat!
HERE WE GO...
COME ON, TREVOR -- DON'T START. YOU'RE DOING THIS FOR ME, REMEMBER.
I KNOW ... I'M NOT. SORRY.
...I'M NOT TOUCHING THIS CHICKEN, THOUGH.
TREVOR!
LUNCH HAS ARRIVED!
Chedd'r Puffs
YOU'RE NOT HAVING ANY CHICKEN, TREVOR?
DON'T YOU LIKE CHICKEN?

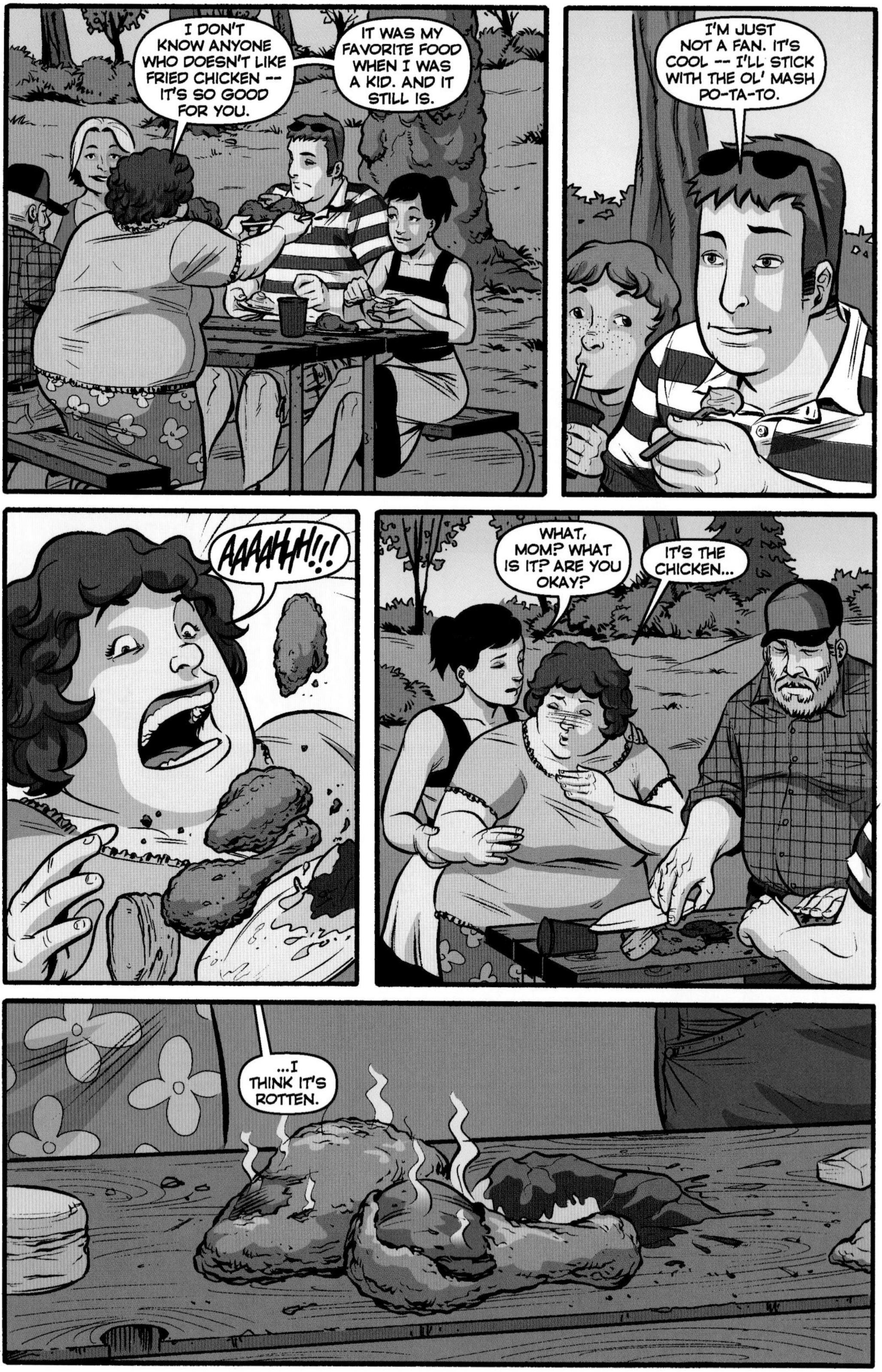
I DON'T KNOW ANYONE WHO DOESN'T LIKE FRIED CHICKEN -- IT'S SO GOOD FOR YOU.
IT WAS MY FAVORITE FOOD WHEN I WAS A KID. AND IT STILL IS.
I'M JUST NOT A FAN. IT'S COOL -- I'LL STICK WITH THE OL' MASH PO-TA-TO.
AAAAHHH!!!
WHAT, MOM? WHAT IS IT? ARE YOU OKAY?
IT'S THE CHICKEN...
...I THINK IT'S ROTTEN.

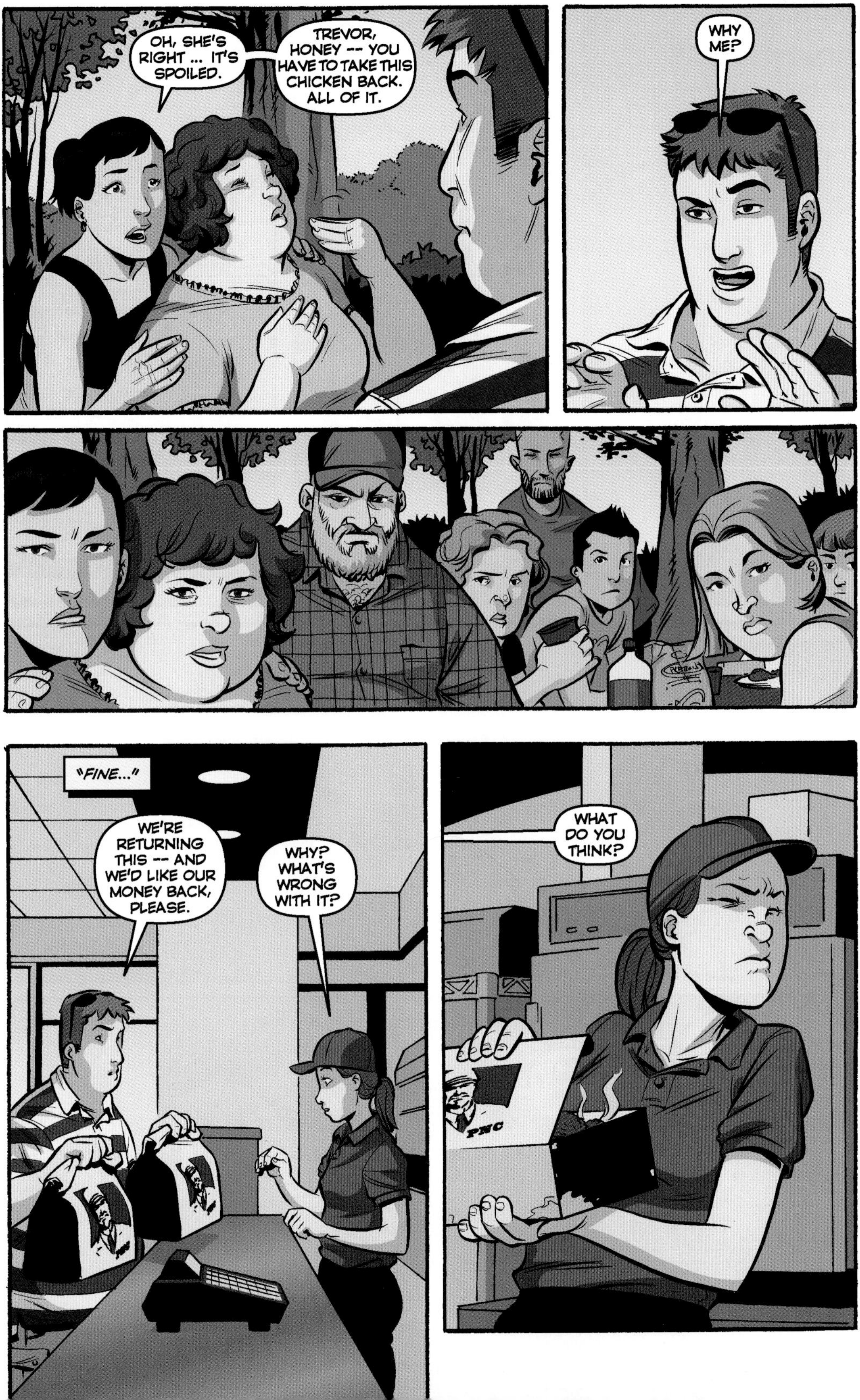
OH, SHE'S RIGHT ... IT'S SPOILED.
TREVOR, HONEY -- YOU HAVE TO TAKE THIS CHICKEN BACK. ALL OF IT.
WHY ME?
"FINE..."
WE'RE RETURNING THIS -- AND WE'D LIKE OUR MONEY BACK, PLEASE.
WHY? WHAT'S WRONG WITH IT?
WHAT DO YOU THINK?
PNC

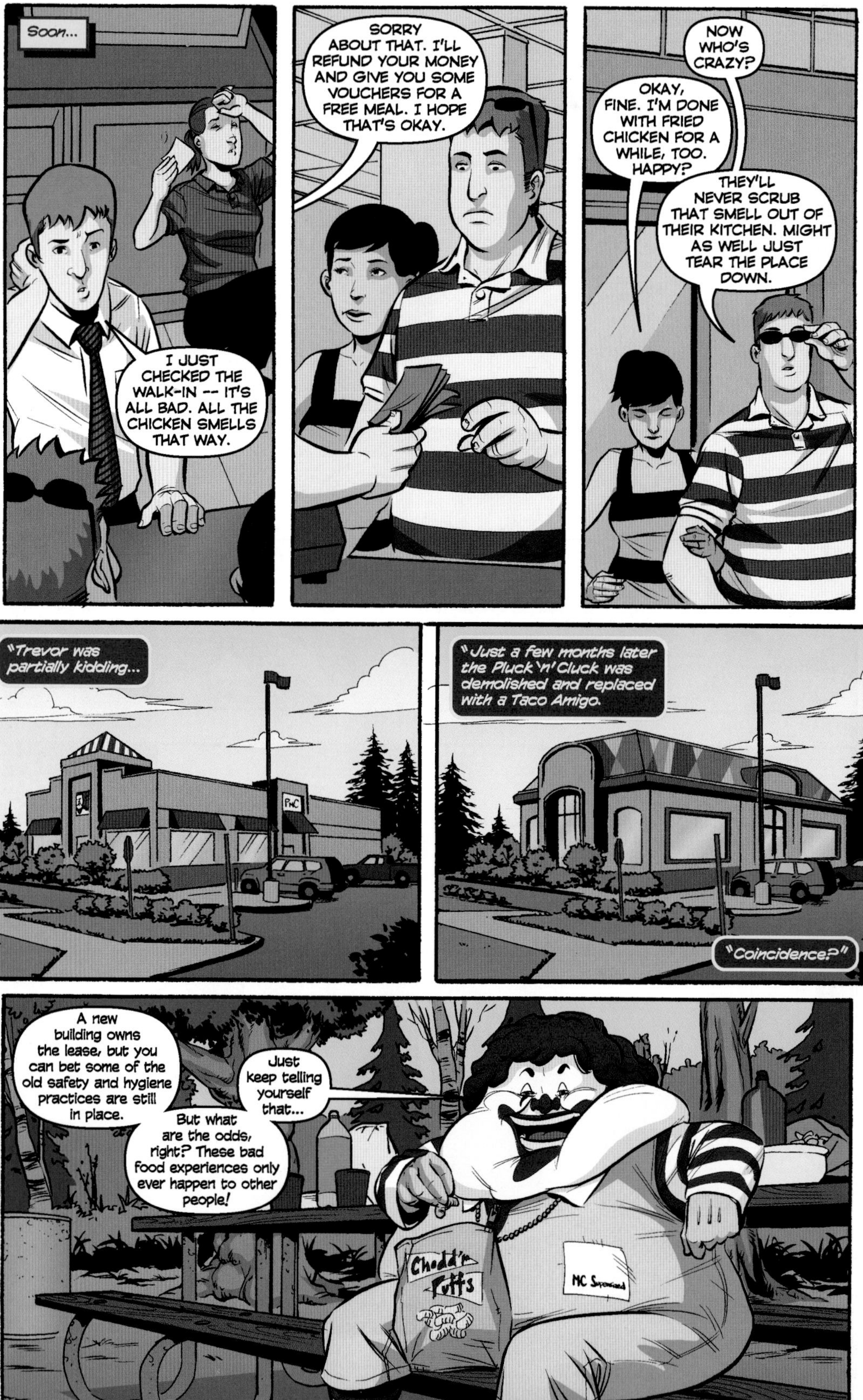
Soon...
I JUST CHECKED THE WALK-IN -- IT'S ALL BAD. ALL THE CHICKEN SMELLS THAT WAY.
SORRY ABOUT THAT. I'LL REFUND YOUR MONEY AND GIVE YOU SOME VOUCHERS FOR A FREE MEAL. I HOPE THAT'S OKAY.
NOW WHO'S CRAZY?
OKAY, FINE. I'M DONE WITH FRIED CHICKEN FOR A WHILE, TOO. HAPPY?
THEY'LL NEVER SCRUB THAT SMELL OUT OF THEIR KITCHEN. MIGHT AS WELL JUST TEAR THE PLACE DOWN.
"Trevor was partially kidding...
PnC
"Just a few months later the Pluck 'n' Cluck was demolished and replaced with a Taco Amigo.
"Coincidence?"
A new building owns the lease, but you can bet some of the old safety and hygiene practices are still in place.
Just keep telling yourself that...
But what are the odds, right? These bad food experiences only ever happen to other people!
Chedd'ar Puffs
MC Supersized

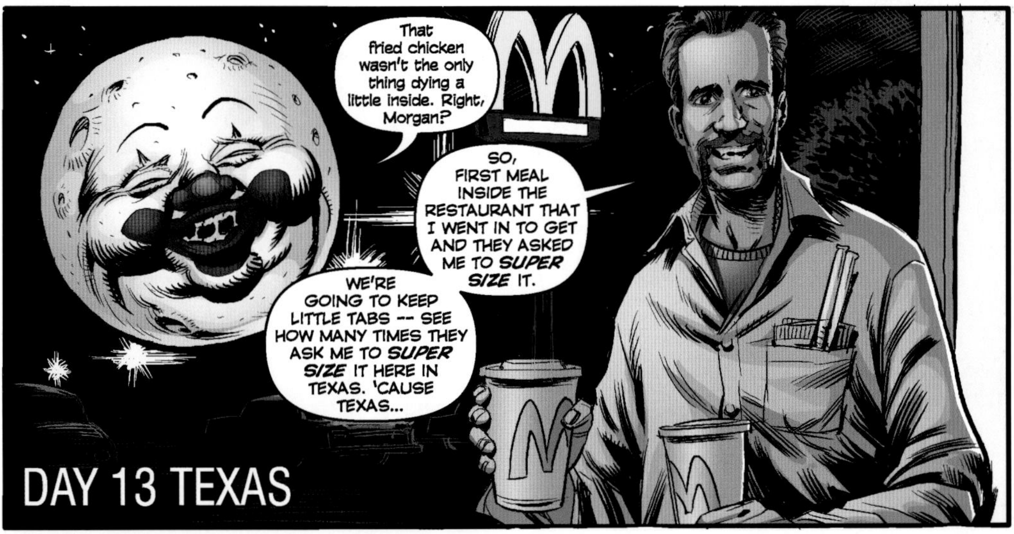
That fried chicken wasn't the only thing dying a little inside. Right, Morgan?
SO, FIRST MEAL INSIDE THE RESTAURANT THAT I WENT IN TO GET AND THEY ASKED ME TO SUPER SIZE IT.
WE'RE GOING TO KEEP LITTLE TABS -- SEE HOW MANY TIMES THEY ASK ME TO SUPER SIZE IT HERE IN TEXAS. 'CAUSE TEXAS...
DAY 13 TEXAS

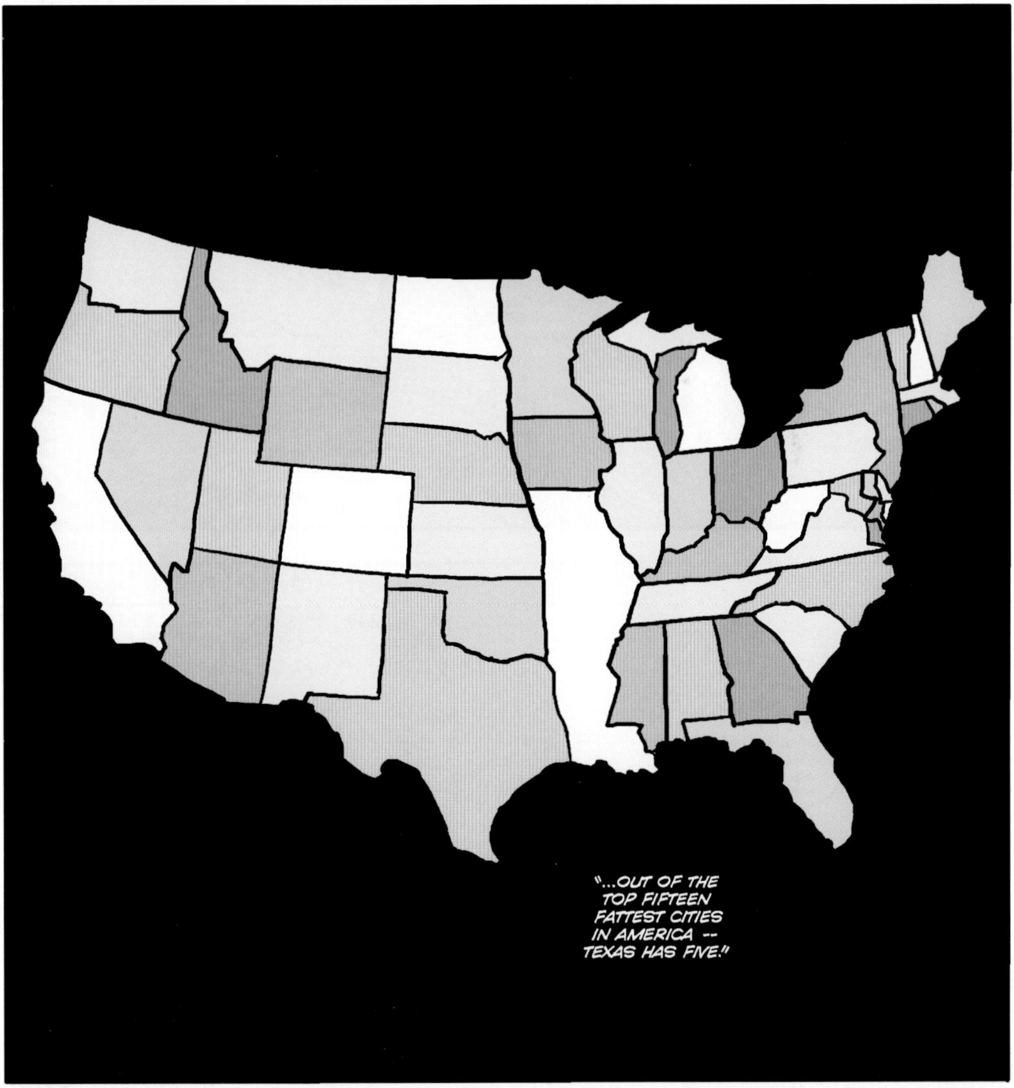
"...OUT OF THE TOP FIFTEEN FATTEST CITIES IN AMERICA -- TEXAS HAS FIVE."

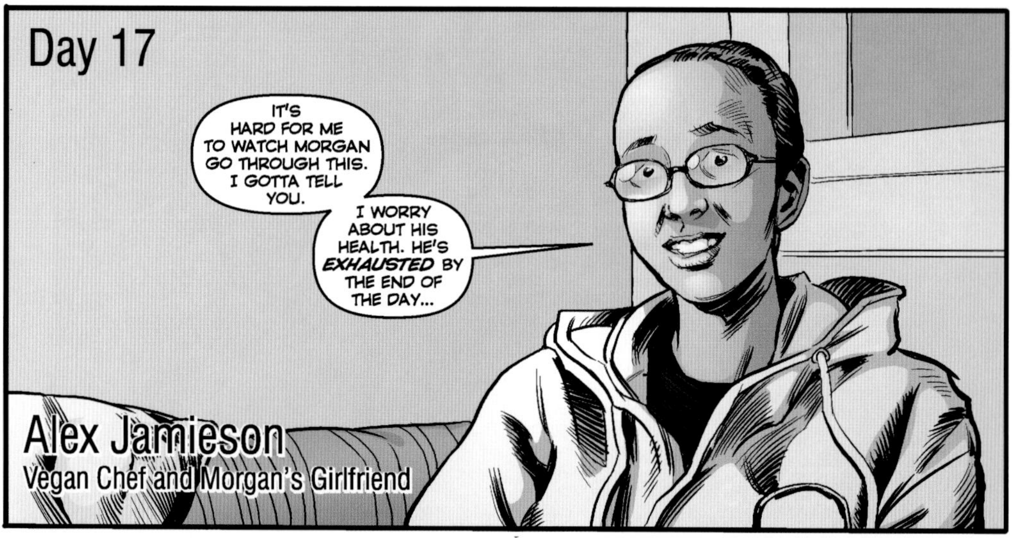
Day 17
IT'S HARD FOR ME TO WATCH MORGAN GO THROUGH THIS. I GOTTA TELL YOU.
I WORRY ABOUT HIS HEALTH. HE'S *EXHAUSTED* BY THE END OF THE DAY...
Alex Jamieson
Vegan Chef and Morgan's Girlfriend

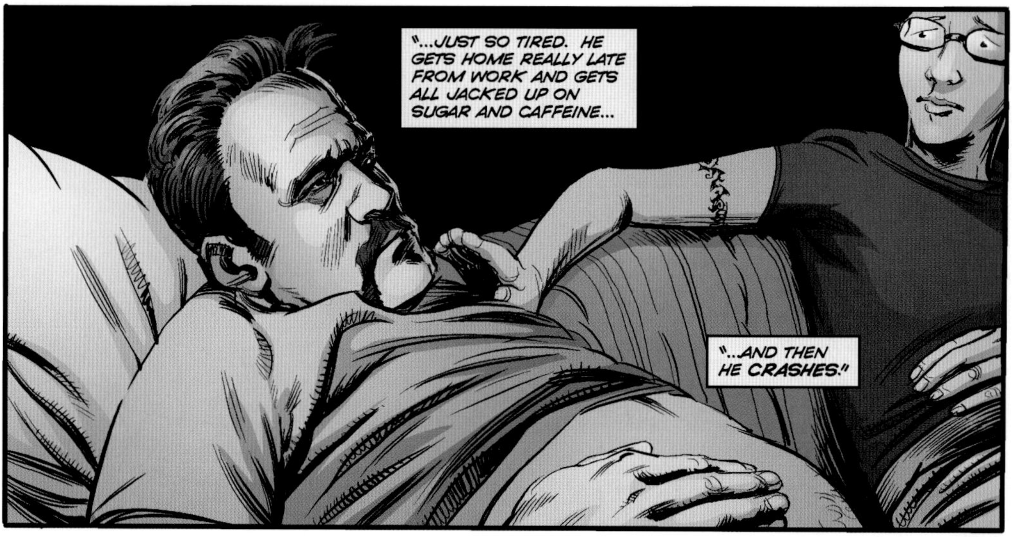
"...JUST SO TIRED. HE GETS HOME REALLY LATE FROM WORK AND GETS ALL JACKED UP ON SUGAR AND CAFFEINE...
"...AND THEN HE *CRASHES*."

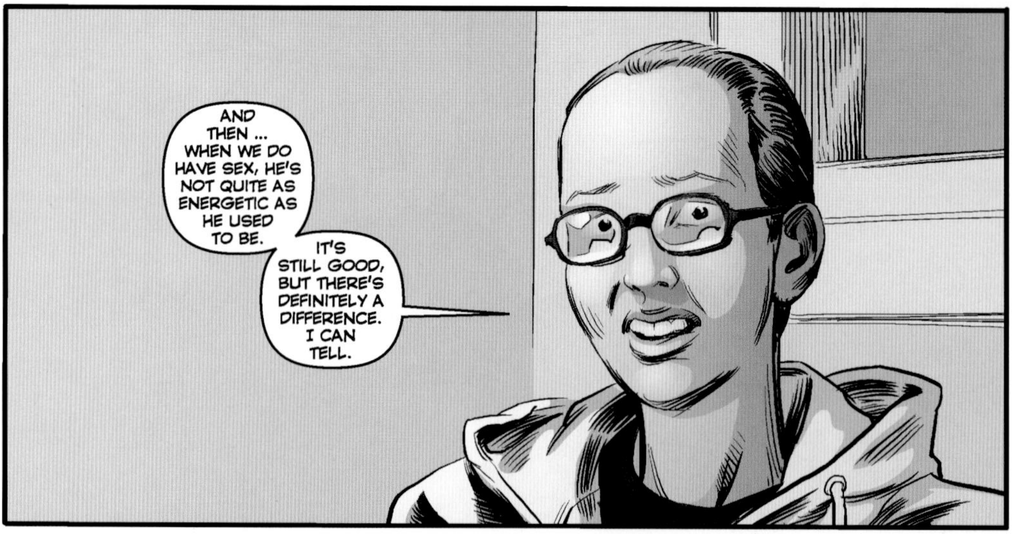
AND THEN ... WHEN WE DO HAVE SEX, HE'S NOT QUITE AS ENERGETIC AS HE USED TO BE.
IT'S STILL GOOD, BUT THERE'S DEFINITELY A DIFFERENCE. I CAN TELL.

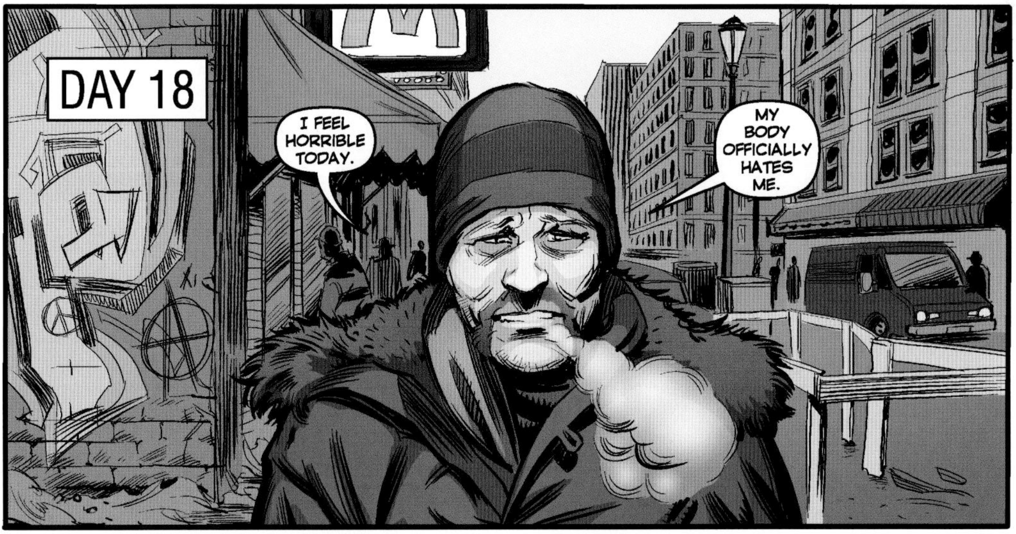
DAY 18
I FEEL HORRIBLE TODAY.
MY BODY OFFICIALLY HATES ME.

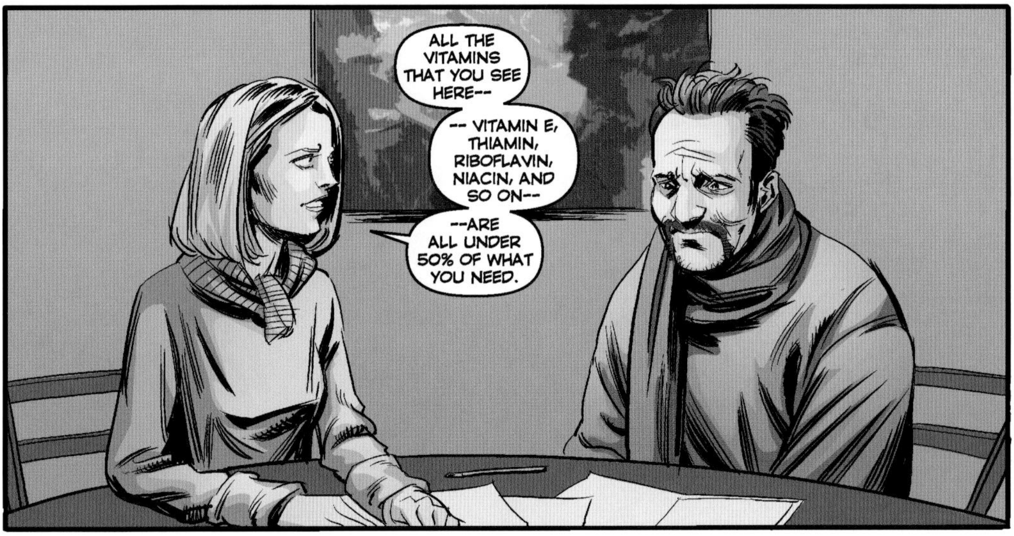
ALL THE VITAMINS THAT YOU SEE HERE--
-- VITAMIN E, THIAMIN, RIBOFLAVIN, NIACIN, AND SO ON--
--ARE ALL UNDER 50% OF WHAT YOU NEED.

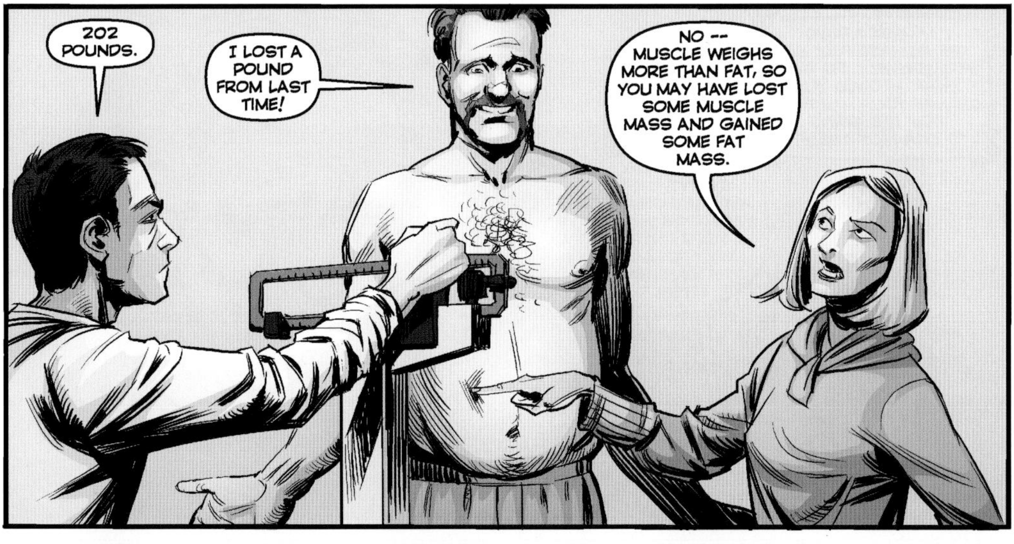
202 POUNDS.
I LOST A POUND FROM LAST TIME!
NO -- MUSCLE WEIGHS MORE THAN FAT, SO YOU MAY HAVE LOST SOME MUSCLE MASS AND GAINED SOME FAT MASS.

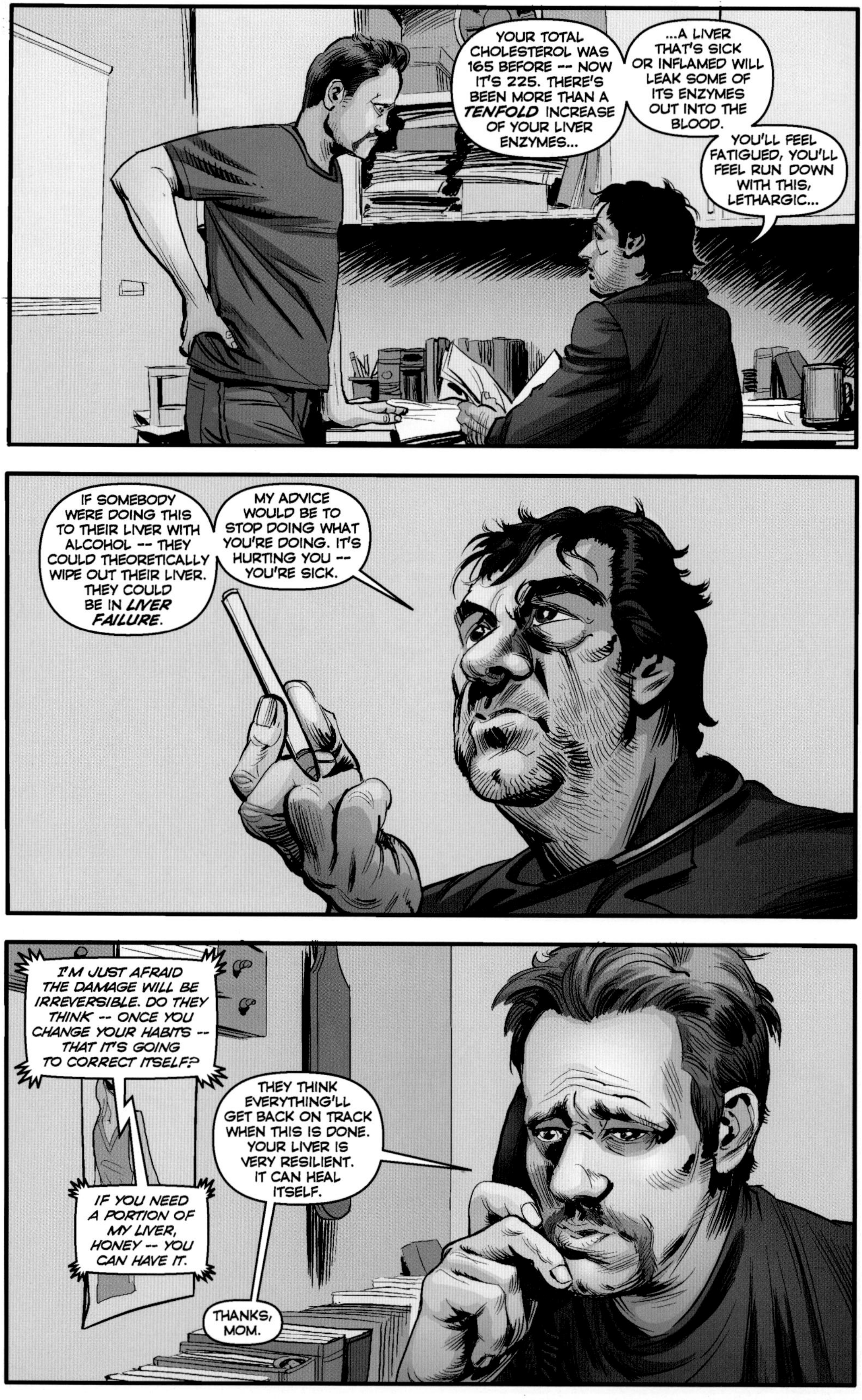
YOUR TOTAL CHOLESTEROL WAS 165 BEFORE -- NOW IT'S 225. THERE'S BEEN MORE THAN A *TENFOLD* INCREASE OF YOUR LIVER ENZYMES...
...A LIVER THAT'S SICK OR INFLAMED WILL LEAK SOME OF ITS ENZYMES OUT INTO THE BLOOD.
YOU'LL FEEL FATIGUED, YOU'LL FEEL RUN DOWN WITH THIS, LETHARGIC...
IF SOMEBODY WERE DOING THIS TO THEIR LIVER WITH ALCOHOL -- THEY COULD THEORETICALLY WIPE OUT THEIR LIVER. THEY COULD BE IN *LIVER FAILURE*.
MY ADVICE WOULD BE TO STOP DOING WHAT YOU'RE DOING. IT'S HURTING YOU -- YOU'RE SICK.
I'M JUST AFRAID THE DAMAGE WILL BE IRREVERSIBLE. DO THEY THINK -- ONCE YOU CHANGE YOUR HABITS -- THAT IT'S GOING TO CORRECT ITSELF?
THEY THINK EVERYTHING'LL GET BACK ON TRACK WHEN THIS IS DONE. YOUR LIVER IS VERY RESILIENT. IT CAN HEAL ITSELF.
IF YOU NEED A PORTION OF MY LIVER, HONEY -- YOU CAN HAVE IT.
THANKS, MOM.

YOUR FRIEND THE FACTORY FARM

A Supersized Instructional Film

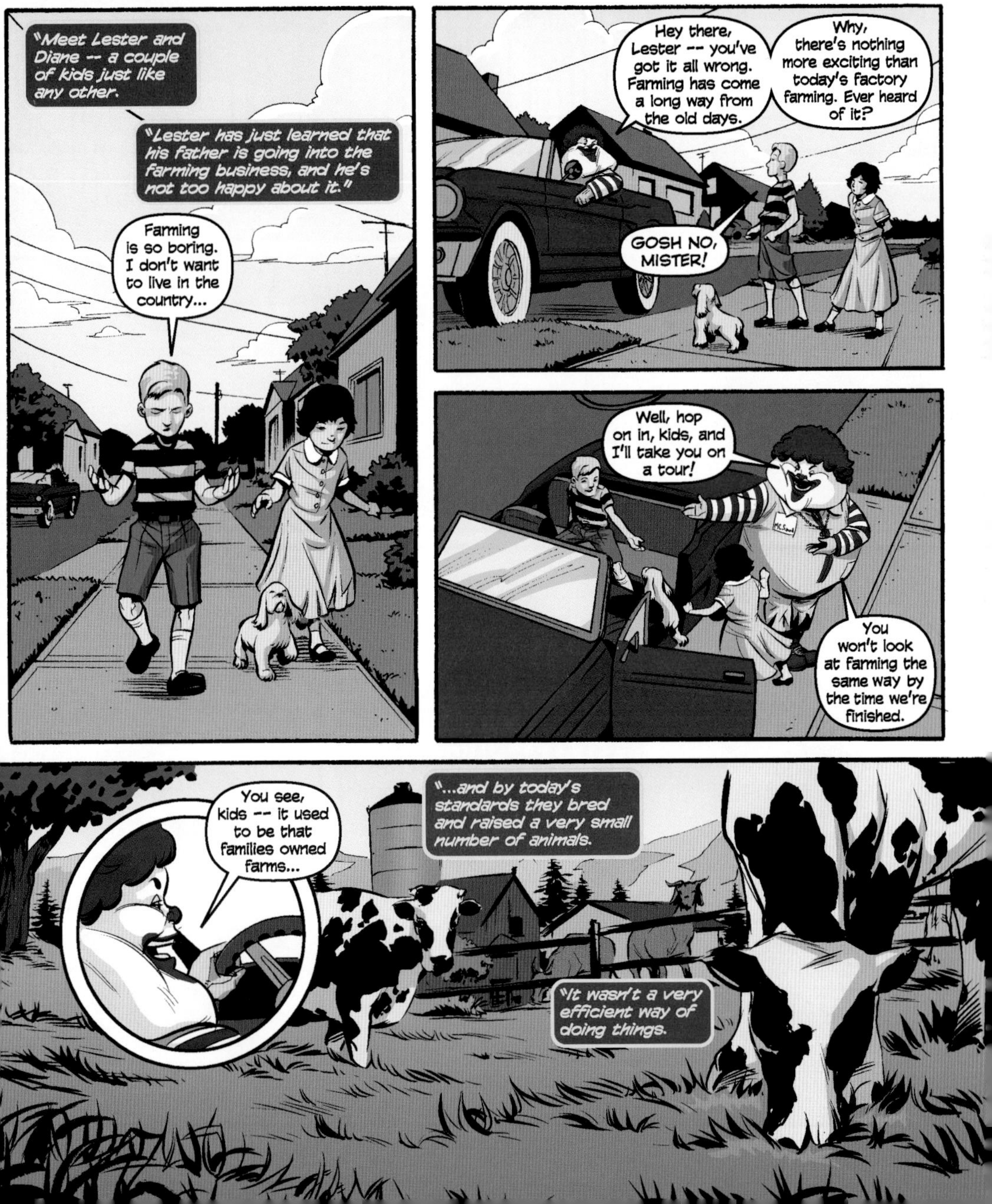
"Meet Lester and Diane -- a couple of kids just like any other.
"Lester has just learned that his father is going into the farming business, and he's not too happy about it."
Farming is so boring. I don't want to live in the country...
Hey there, Lester -- you've got it all wrong. Farming has come a long way from the old days.
Why, there's nothing more exciting than today's factory farming. Ever heard of it?
GOSH NO, MISTER!
Well, hop on in, kids, and I'll take you on a tour!
You won't look at farming the same way by the time we're finished.
You see, kids -- it used to be that families owned farms...
"...and by today's standards they bred and raised a very small number of animals.
"It wasn't a very efficient way of doing things.

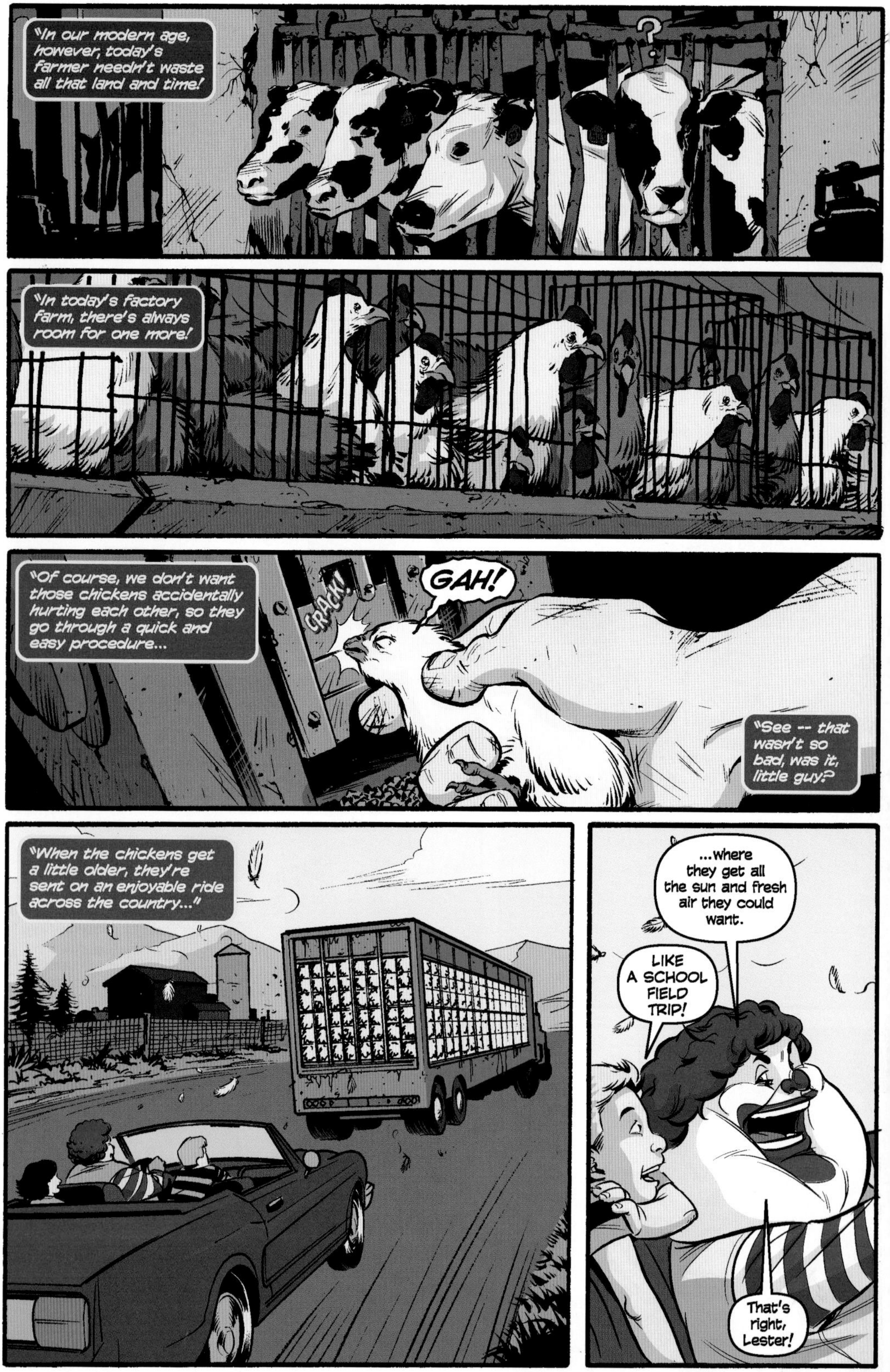
"In our modern age, however, today's farmer needn't waste all that land and time!
"In today's factory farm, there's always room for one more!
"Of course, we don't want those chickens accidentally hurting each other, so they go through a quick and easy procedure...
CRACK!
GAH!
"See -- that wasn't so bad, was it, little guy?
"When the chickens get a little older, they're sent on an enjoyable ride across the country..."
...where they get all the sun and fresh air they could want.
LIKE A SCHOOL FIELD TRIP!
That's right, Lester!

"Their trip brings them to what we call a slaughter-house -- which is a scary name for such a fun place...

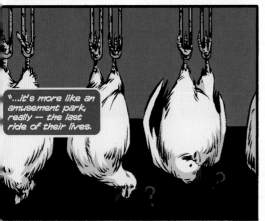

"...it's more like an amusement park, really -- the last ride of their lives.

"First stop is a water park, where a small jolt of harmless electricity relaxes them so they don't feel a thing at the next stop...

"...which is a quick and painless trip through a cutter, so fast that they don't even know what's happening.

"Of course, there are sometimes accidents, but they're dealt with most gently and humanely."

THAT'S GOOD -- ANIMALS SHOULDN'T HAVE TO SUFFER.

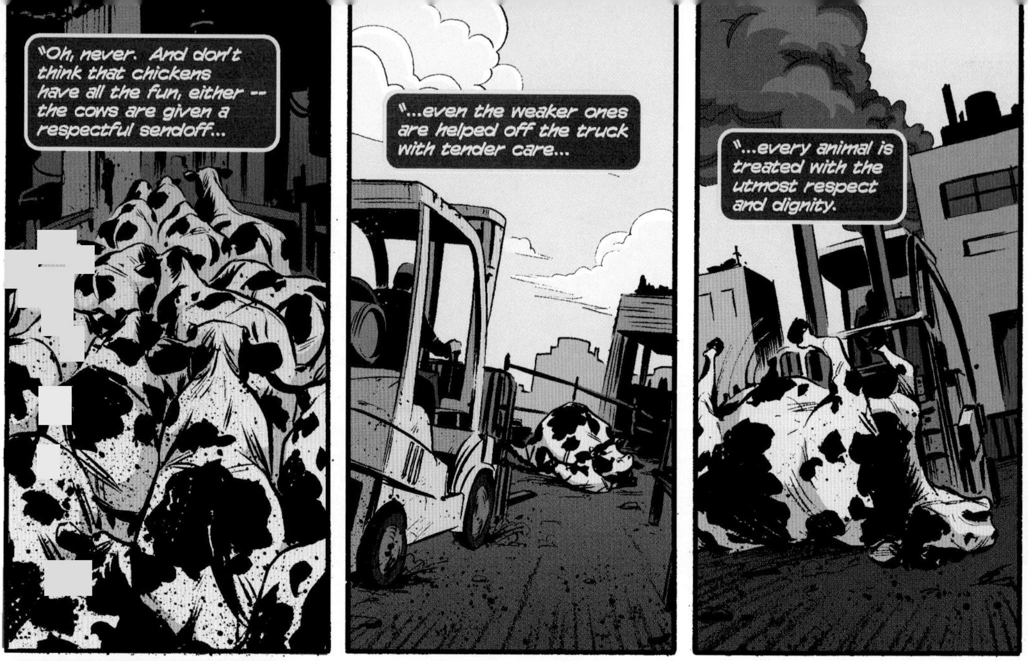
"Oh, never. And don't think that chickens have all the fun, either -- the cows are given a respectful sendoff...
"...even the weaker ones are helped off the truck with tender care...
"...every animal is treated with the utmost respect and dignity.

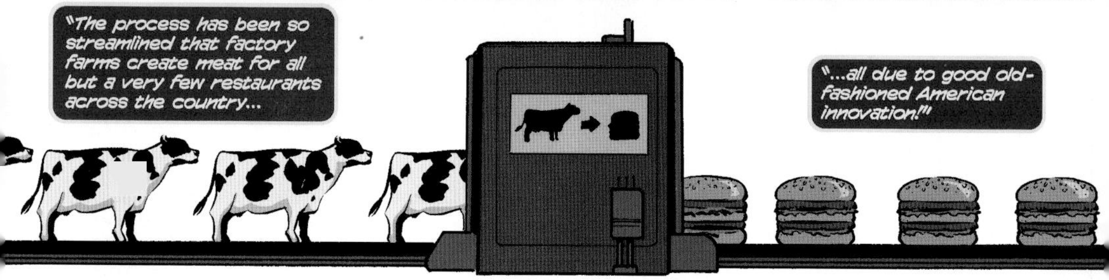
"The process has been so streamlined that factory farms create meat for all but a very few restaurants across the country...
"...all due to good old-fashioned American innovation!"

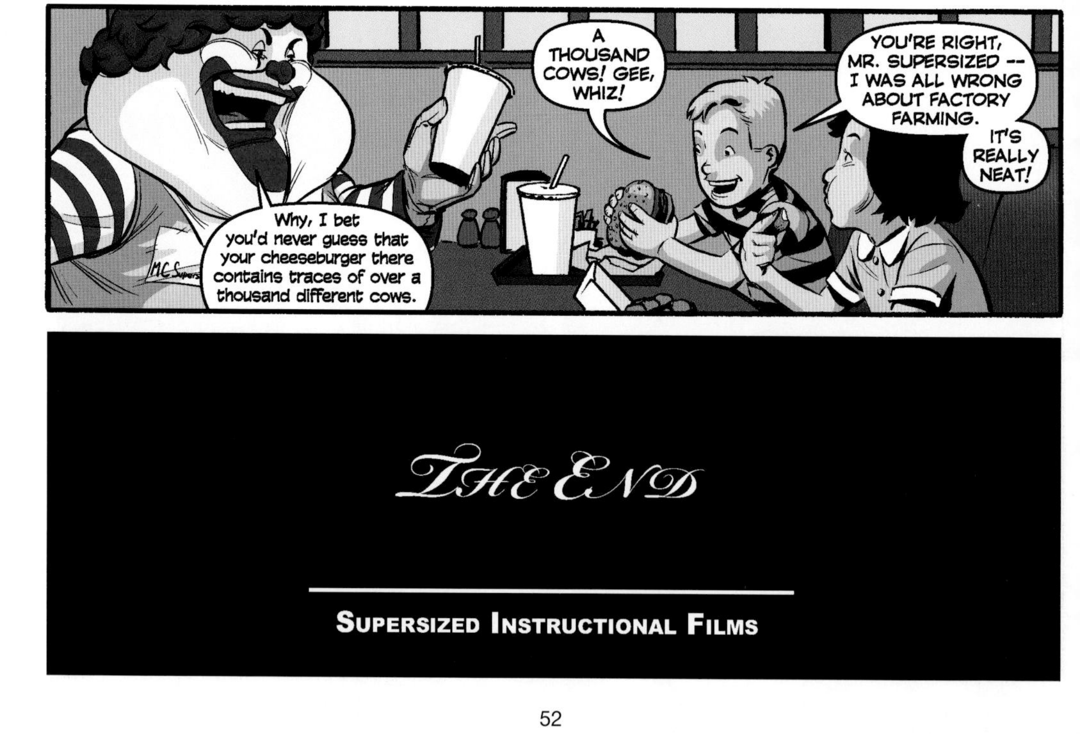
Why, I bet you'd never guess that your cheeseburger there contains traces of over a thousand different cows.
A THOUSAND COWS! GEE, WHIZ!
YOU'RE RIGHT, MR. SUPERSIZED -- I WAS ALL WRONG ABOUT FACTORY FARMING.
IT'S REALLY NEAT!

THE END

Supersized Instructional Films

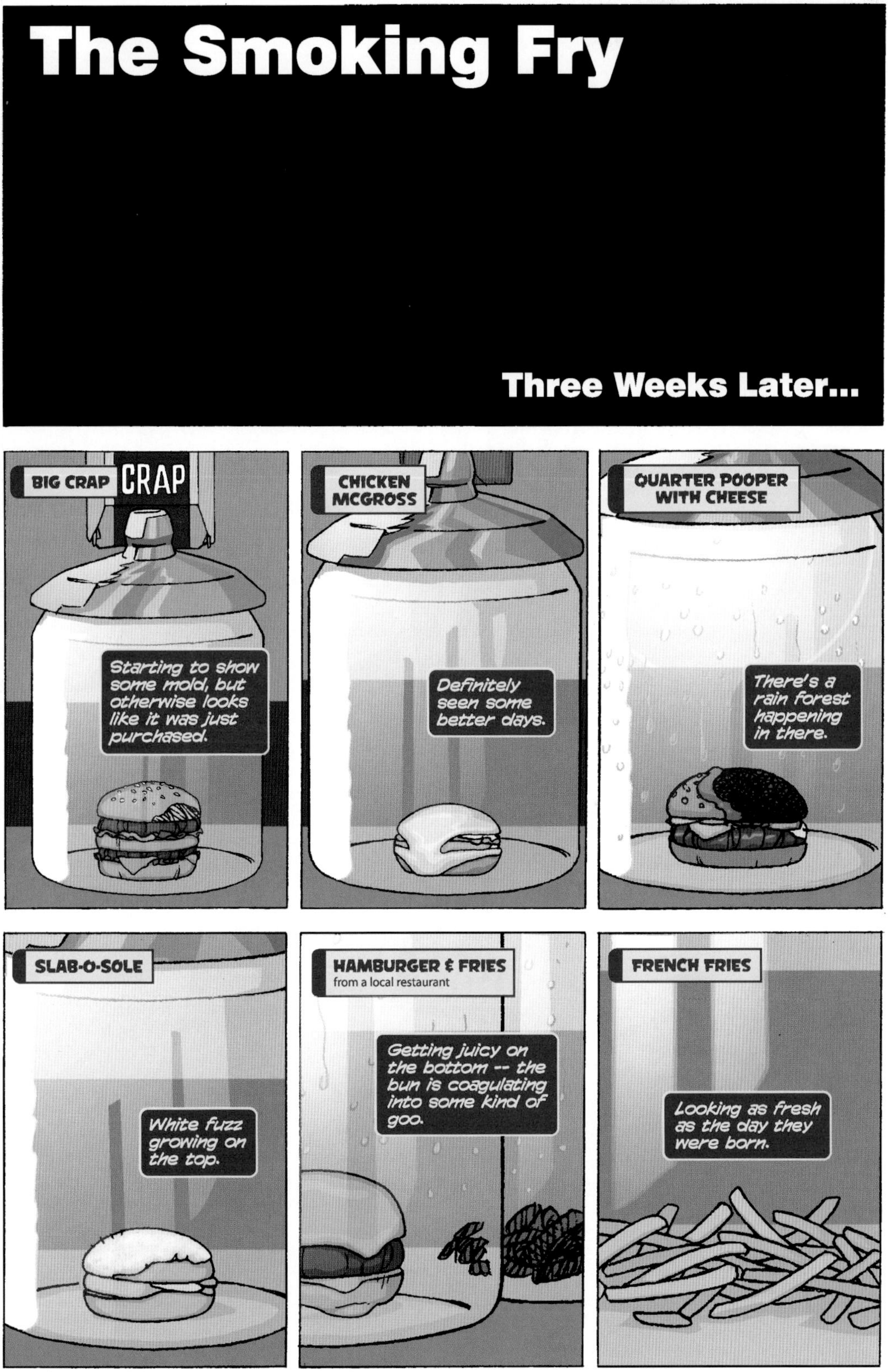
The Smoking Fry
Three Weeks Later...
BIG CRAP
CRAP
Starting to show some mold, but otherwise looks like it was just purchased.
CHICKEN MCGROSS
Definitely seen some better days.
QUARTER POOPER WITH CHEESE
There's a rain forest happening in there.
SLAB-O-SOLE
White fuzz growing on the top.
HAMBURGER & FRIES
from a local restaurant
Getting juicy on the bottom -- the bun is coagulating into some kind of goo.
FRENCH FRIES
Looking as fresh as the day they were born.

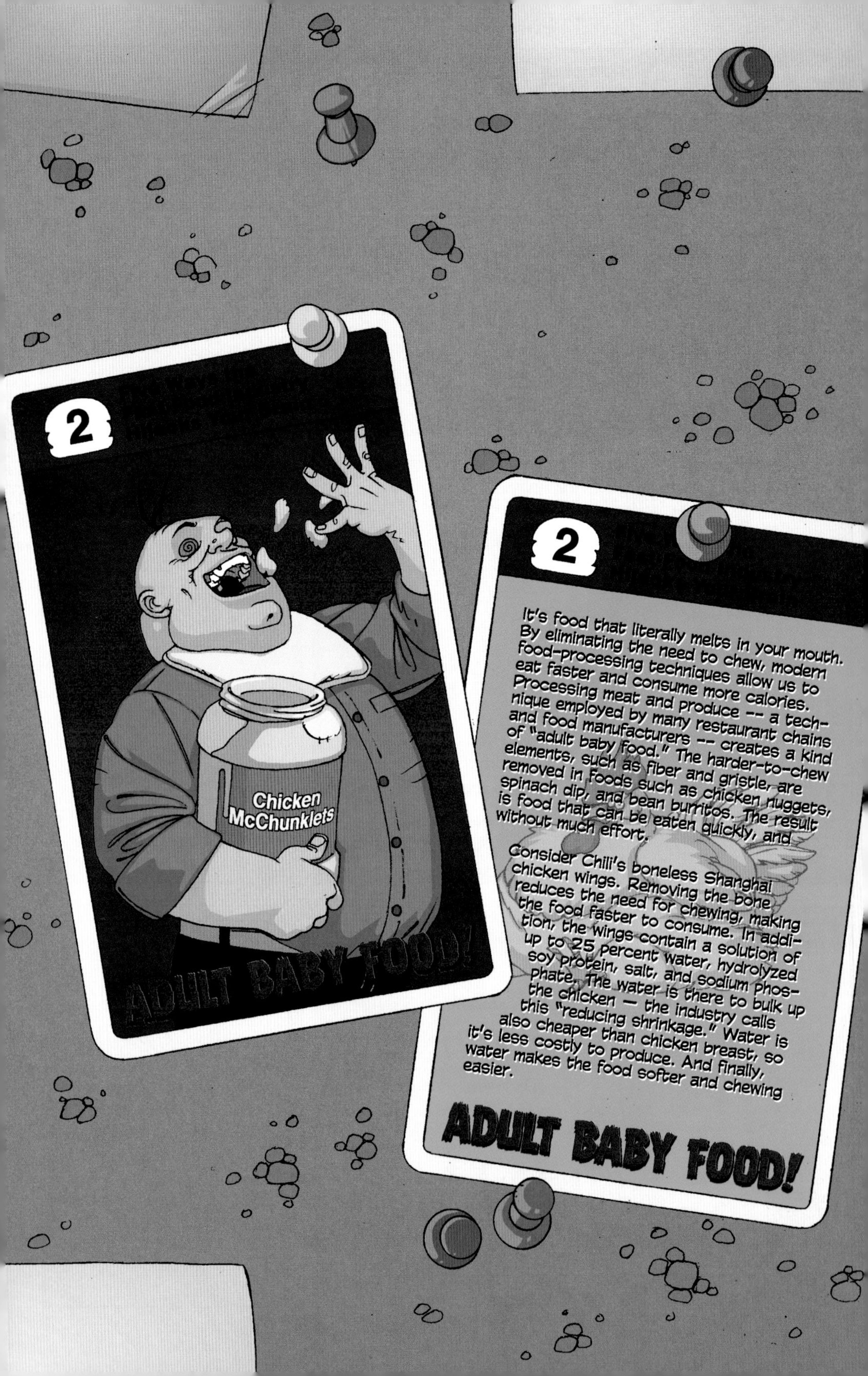
2
Chicken McChunklets
ADULT BABY FOOD!
2
It's food that literally melts in your mouth. By eliminating the need to chew, modern food-processing techniques allow us to eat faster and consume more calories. Processing meat and produce -- a technique employed by many restaurant chains and food manufacturers -- creates a kind of "adult baby food." The harder-to-chew elements, such as fiber and gristle, are removed in foods such as chicken nuggets, spinach dip, and bean burritos. The result is food that can be eaten quickly, and without much effort.
Consider Chili's boneless Shanghai chicken wings. Removing the bone reduces the need for chewing, making the food faster to consume. In addition, the wings contain a solution of up to 25 percent water, hydrolyzed soy protein, salt, and sodium phosphate. The water is there to bulk up the chicken — the industry calls this "reducing shrinkage." Water is also cheaper than chicken breast, so it's less costly to produce. And finally, water makes the food softer and chewing easier.
ADULT BABY FOOD!

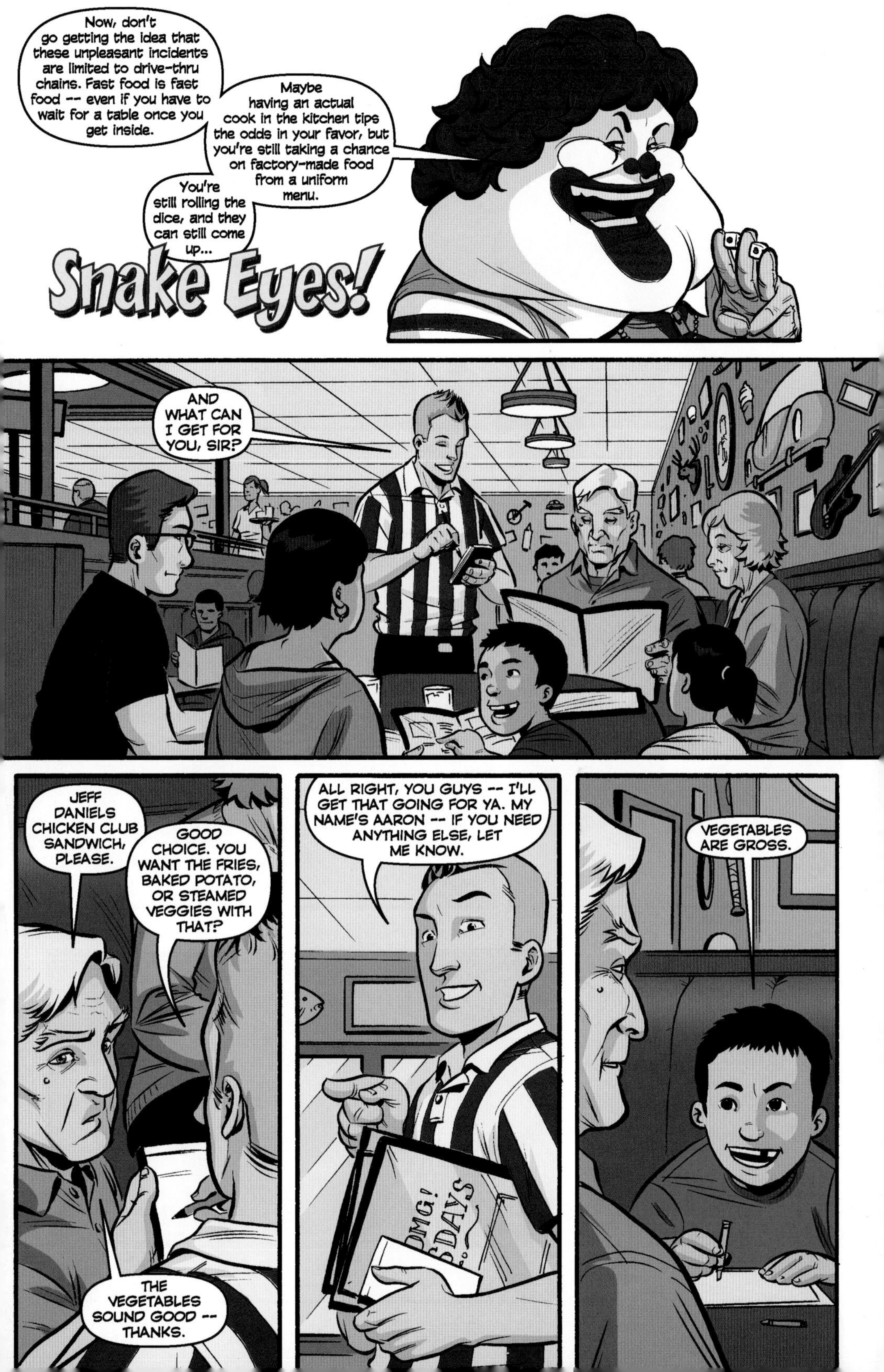
Now, don't go getting the idea that these unpleasant incidents are limited to drive-thru chains. Fast food is fast food -- even if you have to wait for a table once you get inside.
Maybe having an actual cook in the kitchen tips the odds in your favor, but you're still taking a chance on factory-made food from a uniform menu.
You're still rolling the dice, and they can still come up...
Snake Eyes!
AND WHAT CAN I GET FOR YOU, SIR?
JEFF DANIELS CHICKEN CLUB SANDWICH, PLEASE.
GOOD CHOICE. YOU WANT THE FRIES, BAKED POTATO, OR STEAMED VEGGIES WITH THAT?
THE VEGETABLES SOUND GOOD -- THANKS.
ALL RIGHT, YOU GUYS -- I'LL GET THAT GOING FOR YA. MY NAME'S AARON -- IF YOU NEED ANYTHING ELSE, LET ME KNOW.
VEGETABLES ARE GROSS.

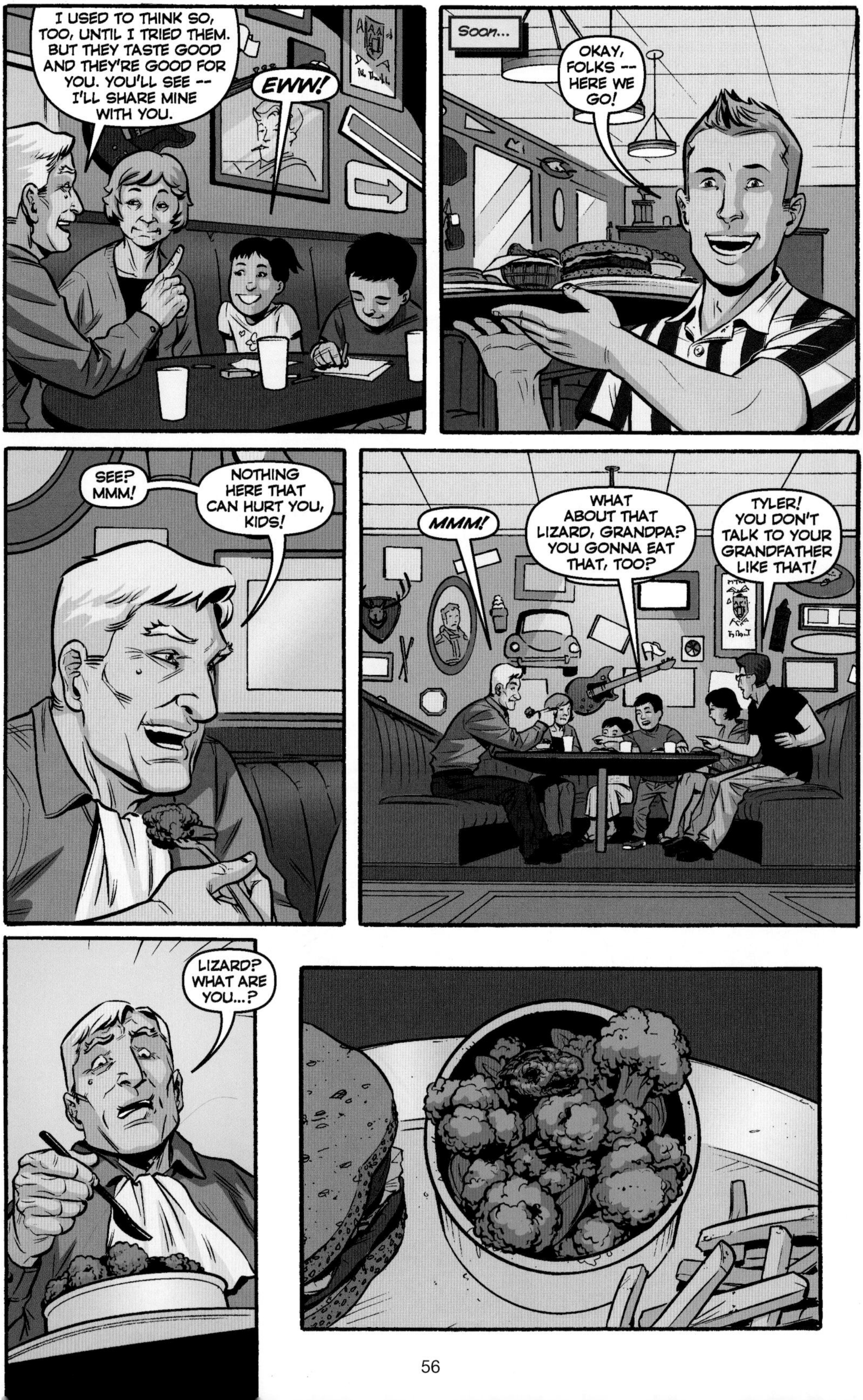
I USED TO THINK SO, TOO, UNTIL I TRIED THEM. BUT THEY TASTE GOOD AND THEY'RE GOOD FOR YOU. YOU'LL SEE -- I'LL SHARE MINE WITH YOU.
EWW!
Soon...
OKAY, FOLKS -- HERE WE GO!
SEE? MMM!
NOTHING HERE THAT CAN HURT YOU, KIDS!
MMM!
WHAT ABOUT THAT LIZARD, GRANDPA? YOU GONNA EAT THAT, TOO?
TYLER! YOU DON'T TALK TO YOUR GRANDFATHER LIKE THAT!
LIZARD? WHAT ARE YOU...?

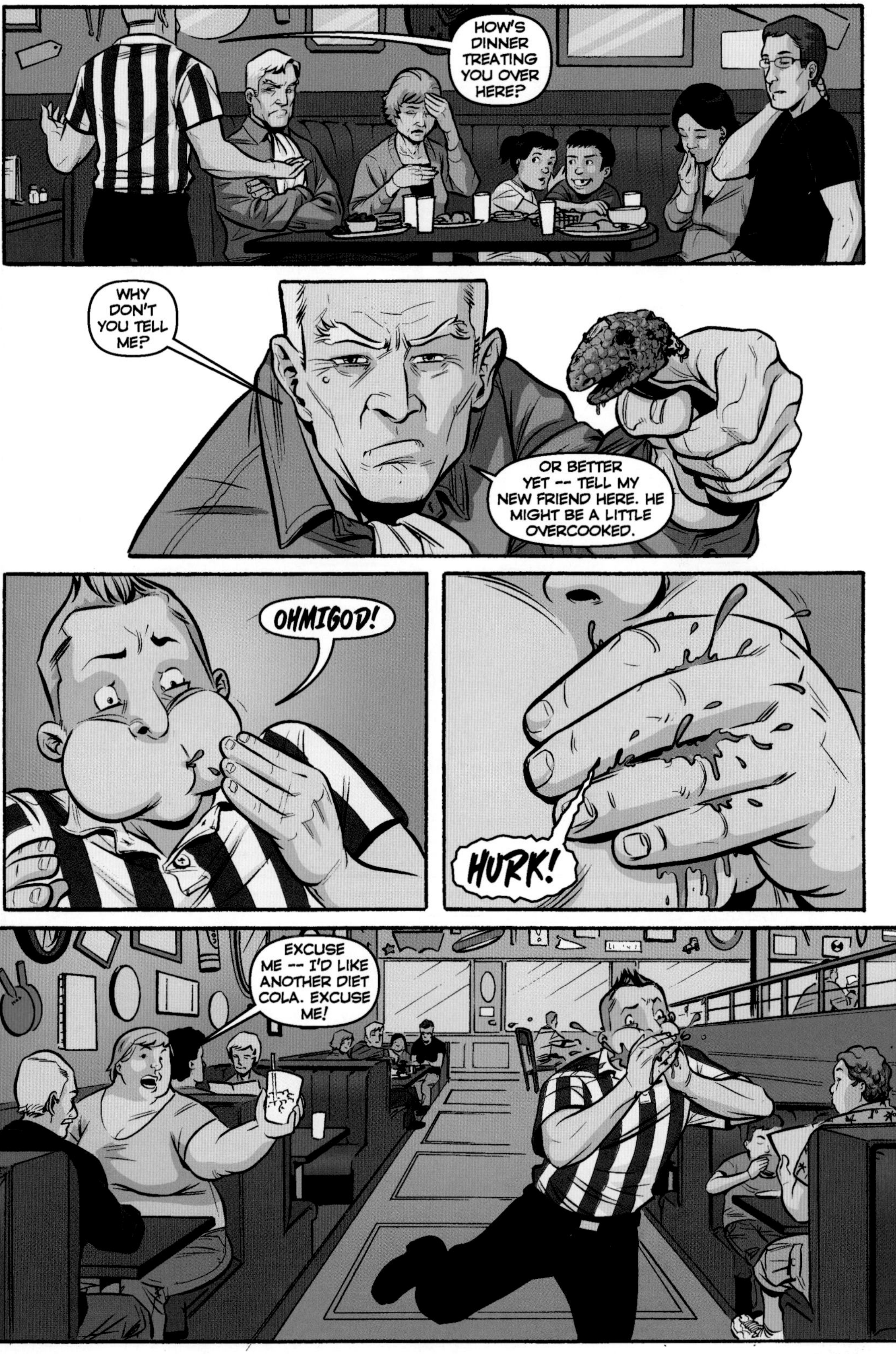
HOW'S DINNER TREATING YOU OVER HERE?
WHY DON'T YOU TELL ME?
OR BETTER YET -- TELL MY NEW FRIEND HERE. HE MIGHT BE A LITTLE OVERCOOKED.
OHMIGOD!
HURK!
EXCUSE ME -- I'D LIKE ANOTHER DIET COLA. EXCUSE ME!

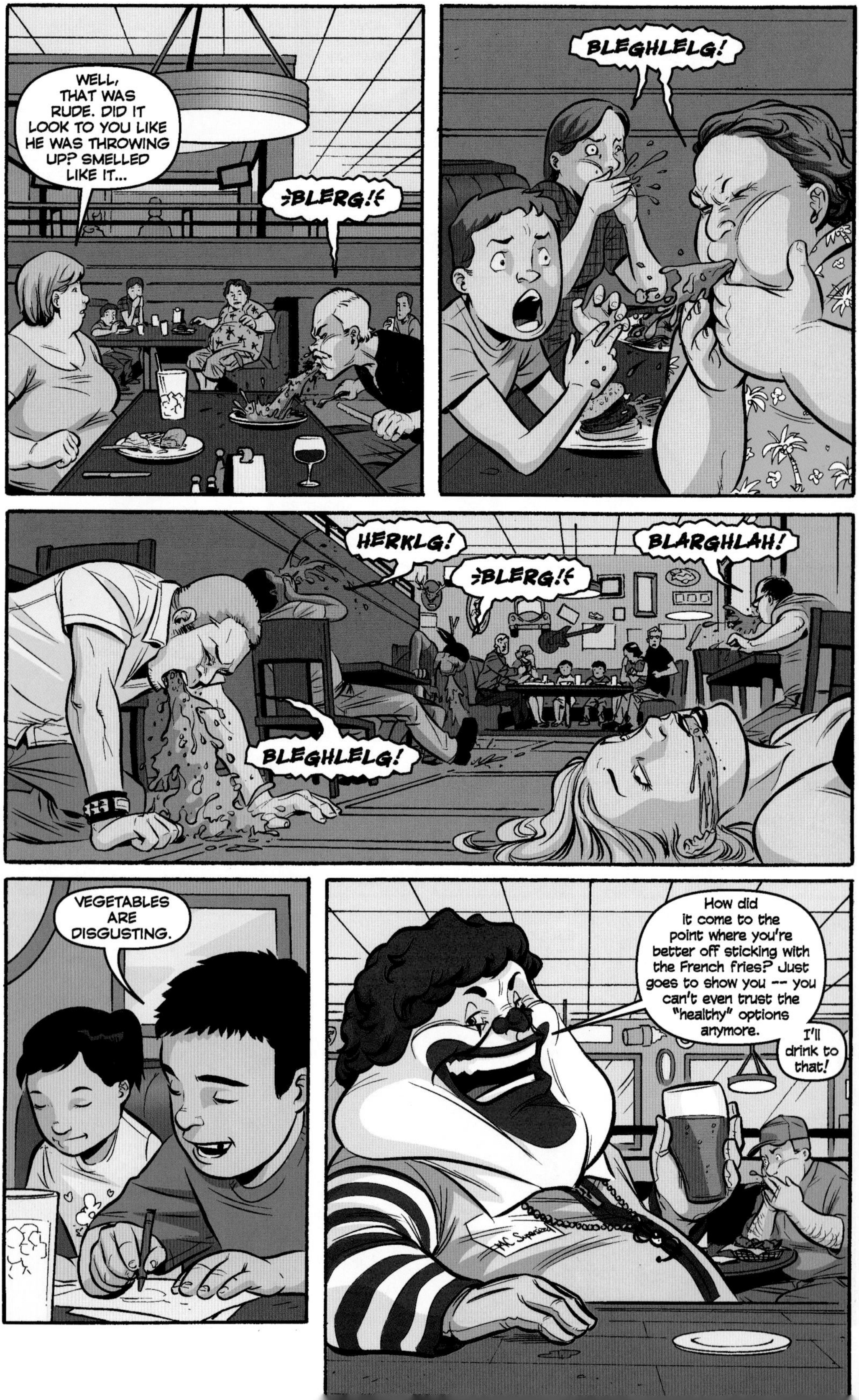
WELL, THAT WAS RUDE. DID IT LOOK TO YOU LIKE HE WAS THROWING UP? SMELLED LIKE IT...
BLERG!
BLEGHLELG!
HERKLG!
BLERG!
BLARGHLAH!
BLEGHLELG!
VEGETABLES ARE DISGUSTING.
How did it come to the point where you're better off sticking with the French fries? Just goes to show you -- you can't even trust the "healthy" options anymore.
I'll drink to that!
MC Supersized

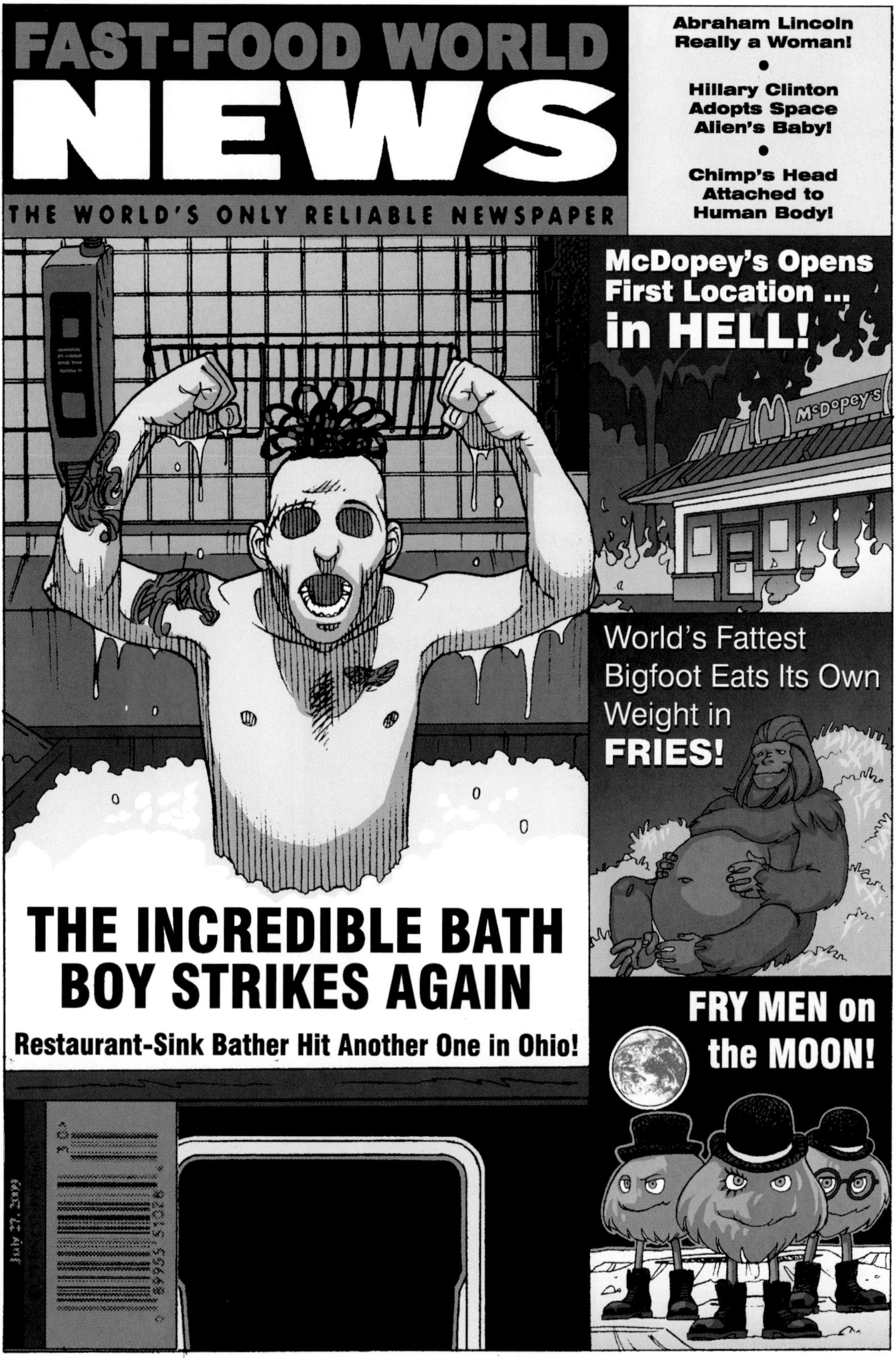
FAST-FOOD WORLD
NEWS
THE WORLD'S ONLY RELIABLE NEWSPAPER
Abraham Lincoln Really a Woman!
Hillary Clinton Adopts Space Alien's Baby!
Chimp's Head Attached to Human Body!
McDopey's Opens First Location ... in HELL!
McDopey's
World's Fattest Bigfoot Eats Its Own Weight in FRIES!
THE INCREDIBLE BATH BOY STRIKES AGAIN
Restaurant-Sink Bather Hit Another One in Ohio!
FRY MEN on the MOON!

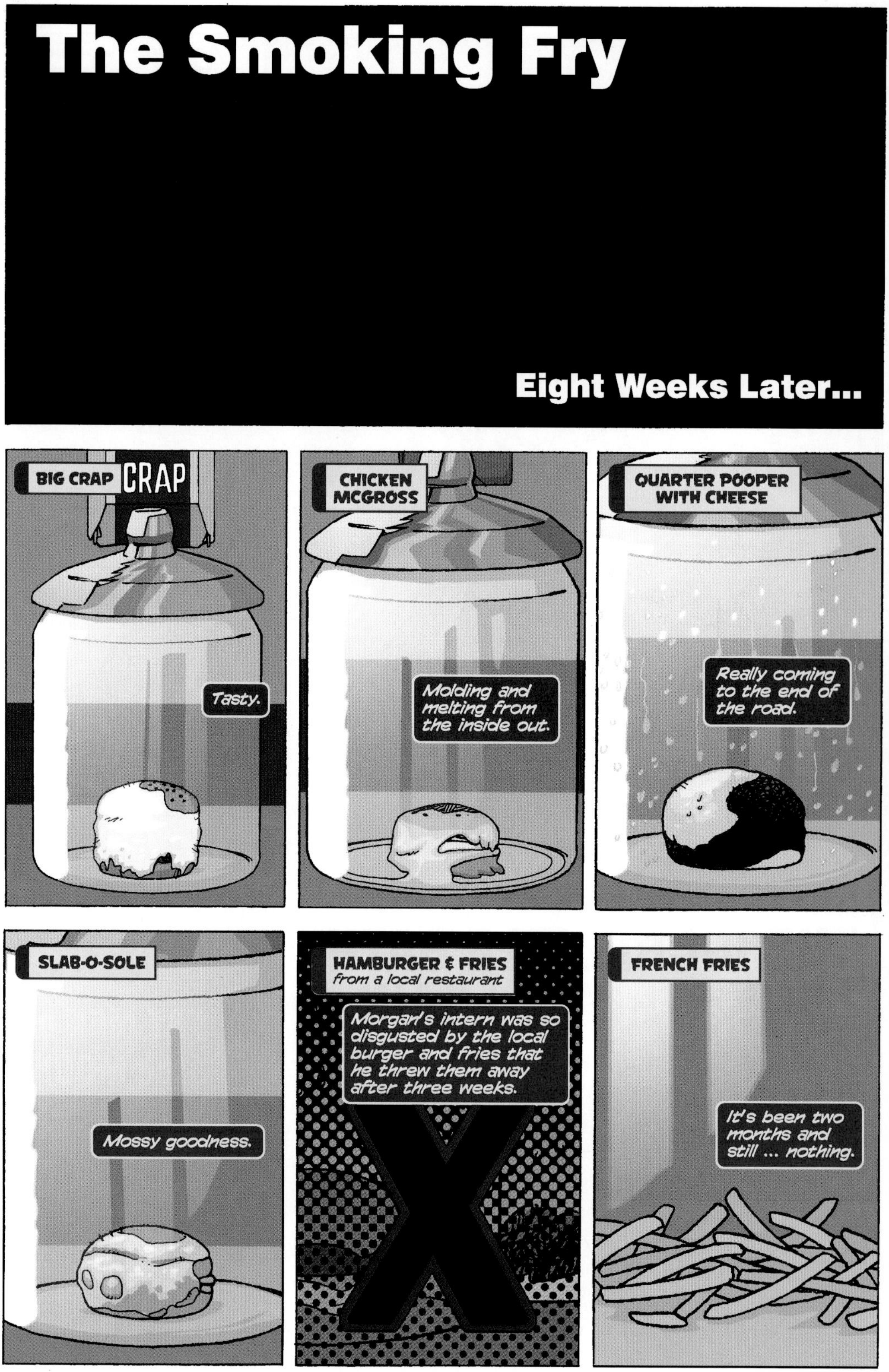
The Smoking Fry
Eight Weeks Later...
BIG CRAP
CRAP
Tasty.
CHICKEN MCGROSS
Molding and melting from the inside out.
QUARTER POOPER WITH CHEESE
Really coming to the end of the road.
SLAB-O-SOLE
Mossy goodness.
HAMBURGER & FRIES
from a local restaurant
Morgan's intern was so disgusted by the local burger and fries that he threw them away after three weeks.
FRENCH FRIES
It's been two months and still ... nothing.

Day 21 -- 2:00 a.m.

"Meanwhile, things are going just about as well with Morgan and his McDopey's diet..."

IT'S TWO A.M. ... I WOKE UP HAVING DIFFICULTY BREATHING. I'M VERY HOT. FELT LIKE I WAS HAVING HEART PALPITATIONS.

CAME UP AND WALKED AROUND THE LIVING ROOM, TRYING TO GET MY BREATH BACK.

I WANT TO FINISH, BUT I DON'T WANT ANYTHING *BAD* TO HAPPEN, EITHER.

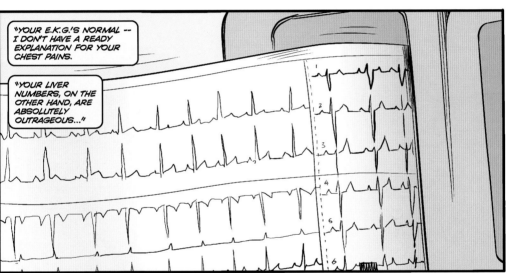

"YOUR E.K.G.'S NORMAL -- I DON'T HAVE A READY EXPLANATION FOR YOUR CHEST PAINS.

"YOUR LIVER NUMBERS, ON THE OTHER HAND, ARE ABSOLUTELY OUTRAGEOUS..."

...YOU'RE GIVING YOURSELF *HYPERURICEMIA.* THE DANGER WITH THAT IS GOUT, KIDNEY STONES...

THE RESULTS FOR YOUR LIVER ARE *OBSCENE* BEYOND ANYTHING I WOULD HAVE THOUGHT.

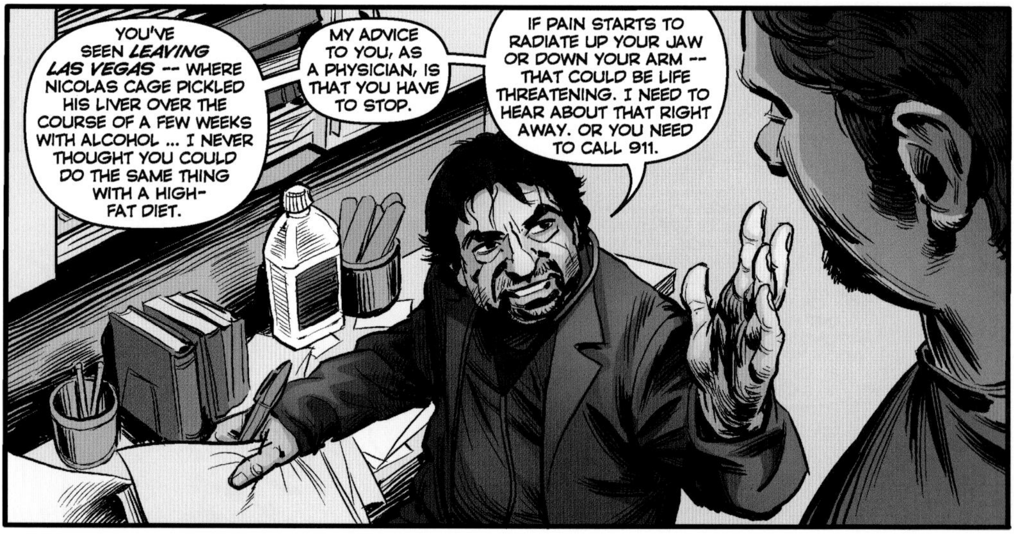
YOU'VE SEEN *LEAVING LAS VEGAS* -- WHERE NICOLAS CAGE PICKLED HIS LIVER OVER THE COURSE OF A FEW WEEKS WITH ALCOHOL ... I NEVER THOUGHT YOU COULD DO THE SAME THING WITH A HIGH-FAT DIET.
MY ADVICE TO YOU, AS A PHYSICIAN, IS THAT YOU HAVE TO STOP.
IF PAIN STARTS TO RADIATE UP YOUR JAW OR DOWN YOUR ARM -- THAT COULD BE LIFE THREATENING. I NEED TO HEAR ABOUT THAT RIGHT AWAY. OR YOU NEED TO CALL 911.

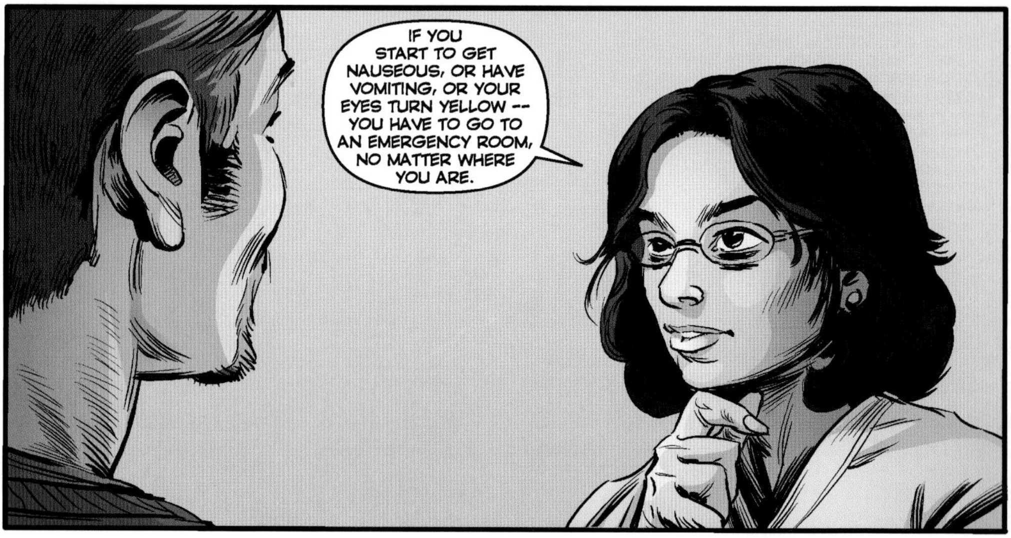
IF YOU START TO GET NAUSEOUS, OR HAVE VOMITING, OR YOUR EYES TURN YELLOW -- YOU HAVE TO GO TO AN EMERGENCY ROOM, NO MATTER WHERE YOU ARE.

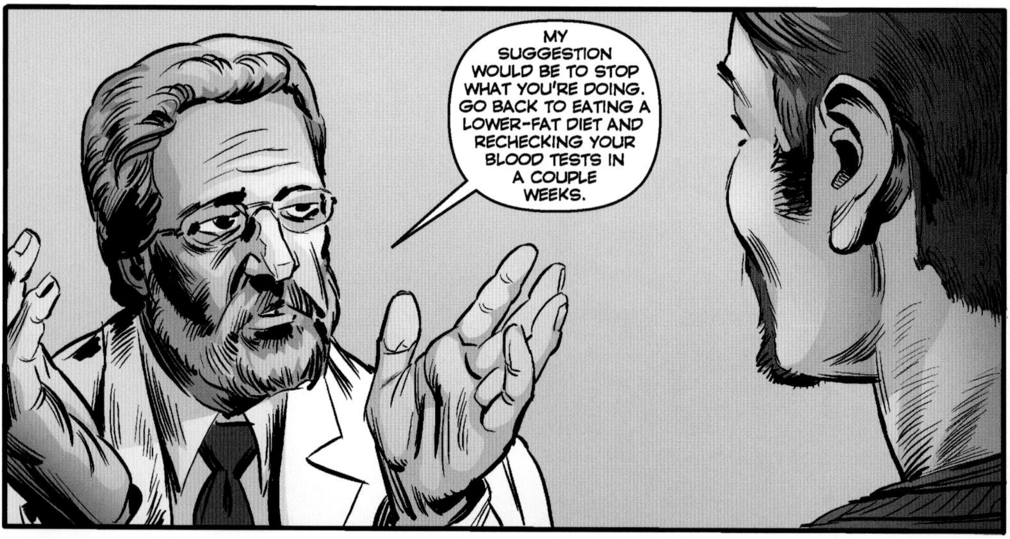
MY SUGGESTION WOULD BE TO STOP WHAT YOU'RE DOING. GO BACK TO EATING A LOWER-FAT DIET AND RECHECKING YOUR BLOOD TESTS IN A COUPLE WEEKS.

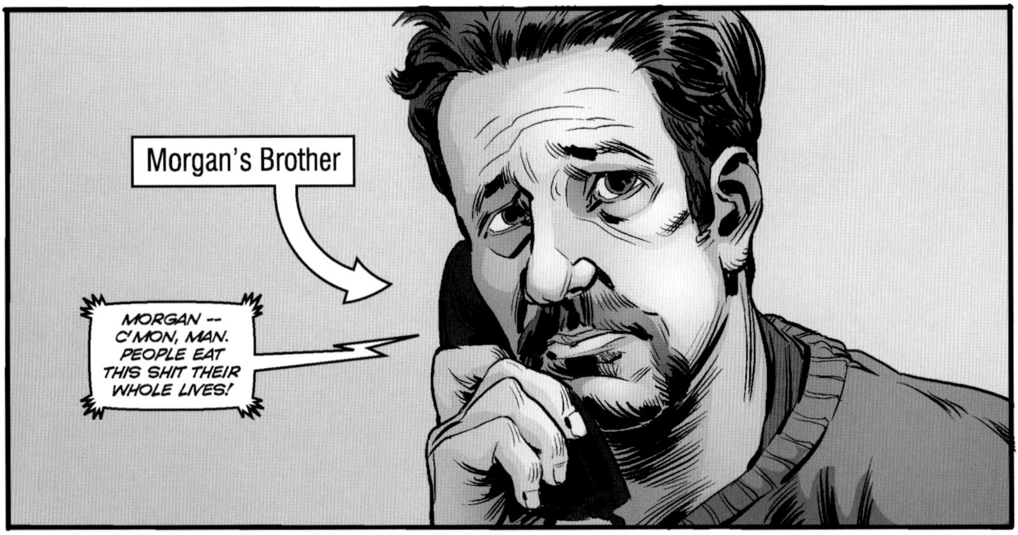
Morgan's Brother
MORGAN -- C'MON, MAN. PEOPLE EAT THIS SHIT THEIR WHOLE LIVES!

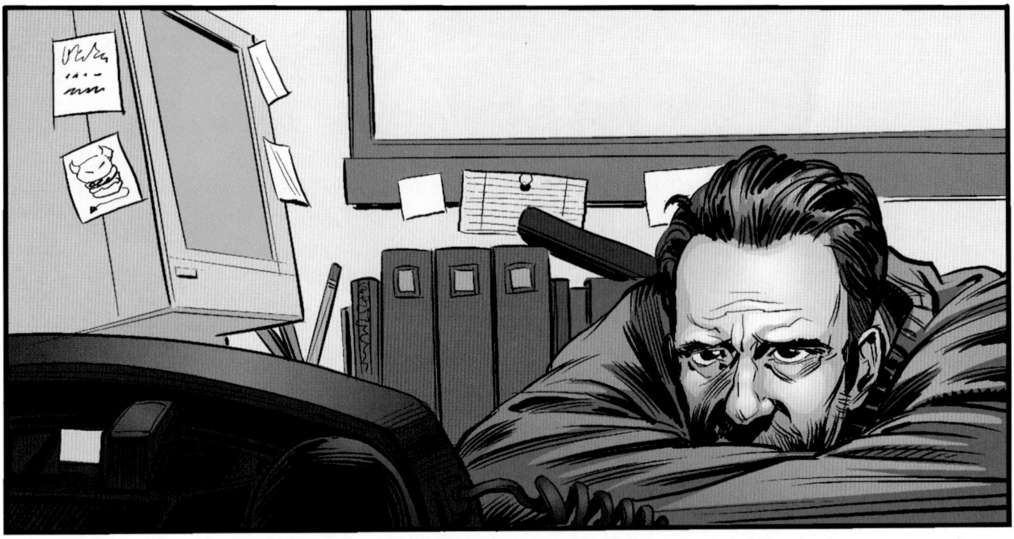

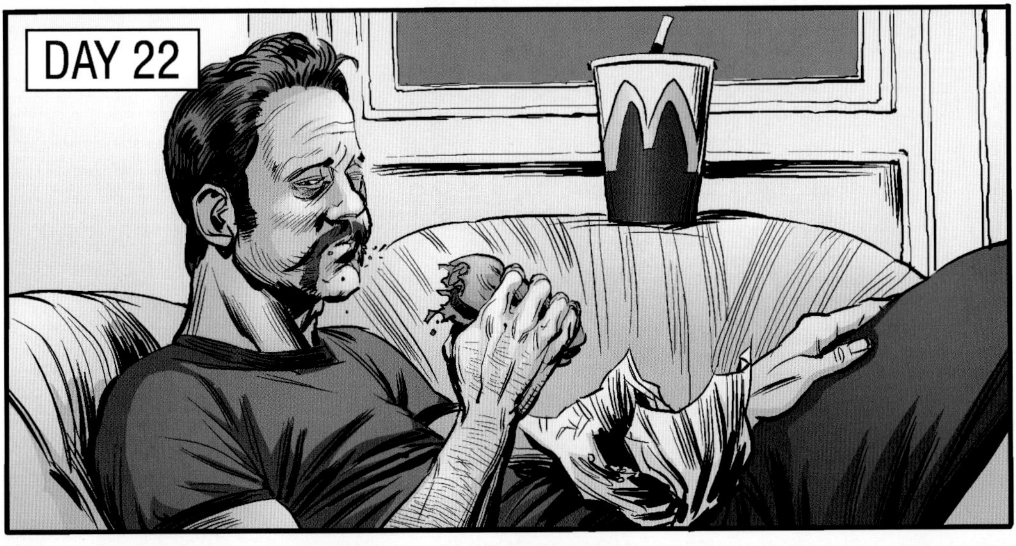
DAY 22

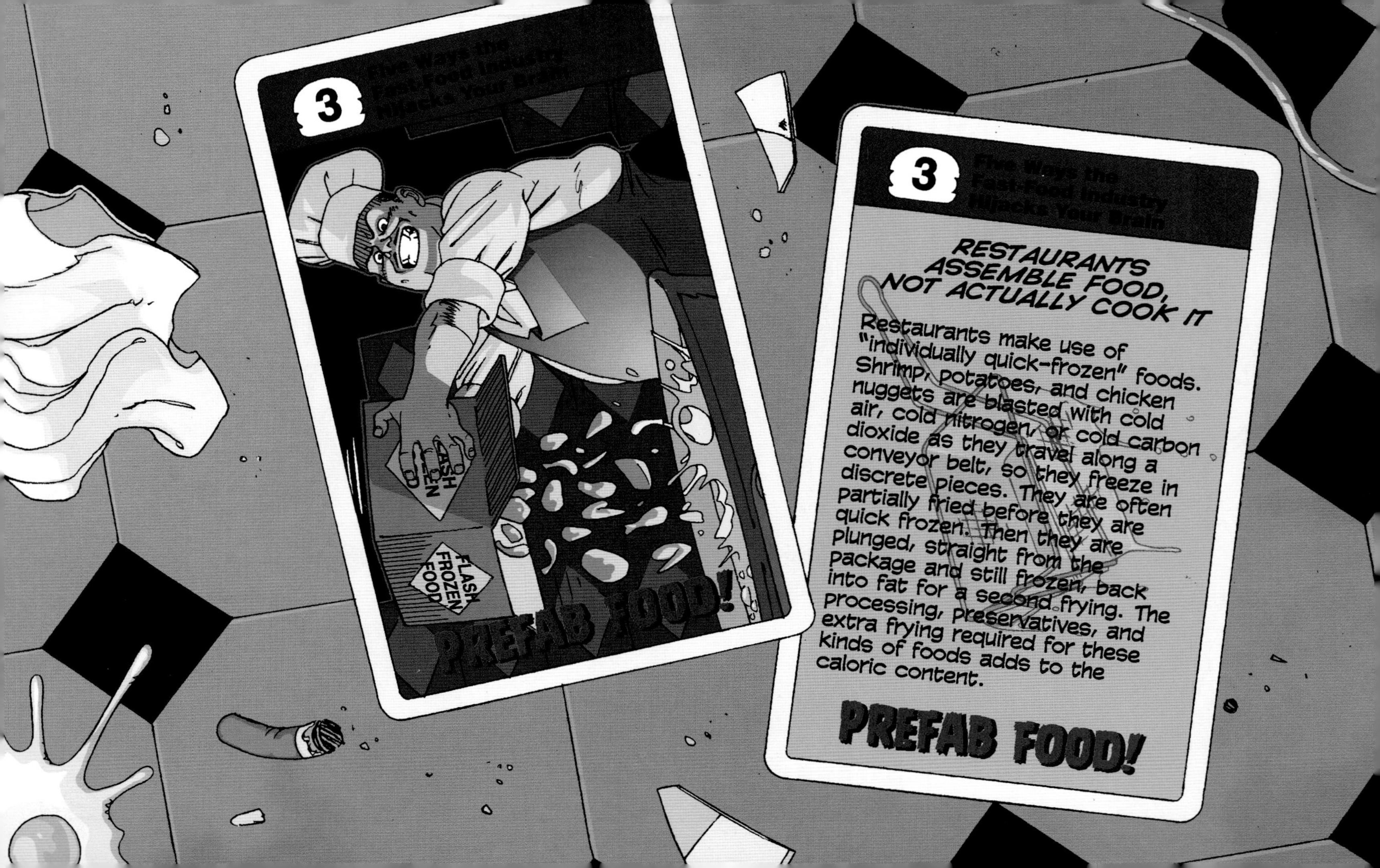
3
Five Ways the Fast-Food Industry Hijacks Your Brain
FLASH FROZEN FOOD
FLASH FROZEN FOOD
PREFAB FOOD!
3
Five Ways the Fast-Food Industry Hijacks Your Brain
RESTAURANTS ASSEMBLE FOOD, NOT ACTUALLY COOK IT
Restaurants make use of "individually quick-frozen" foods. Shrimp, potatoes, and chicken nuggets are blasted with cold air, cold nitrogen, or cold carbon dioxide as they travel along a conveyor belt, so they freeze in discrete pieces. They are often partially fried before they are quick frozen. Then they are plunged, straight from the package and still frozen, back into fat for a second frying. The processing, preservatives, and extra frying required for these kinds of foods adds to the caloric content.
PREFAB FOOD!

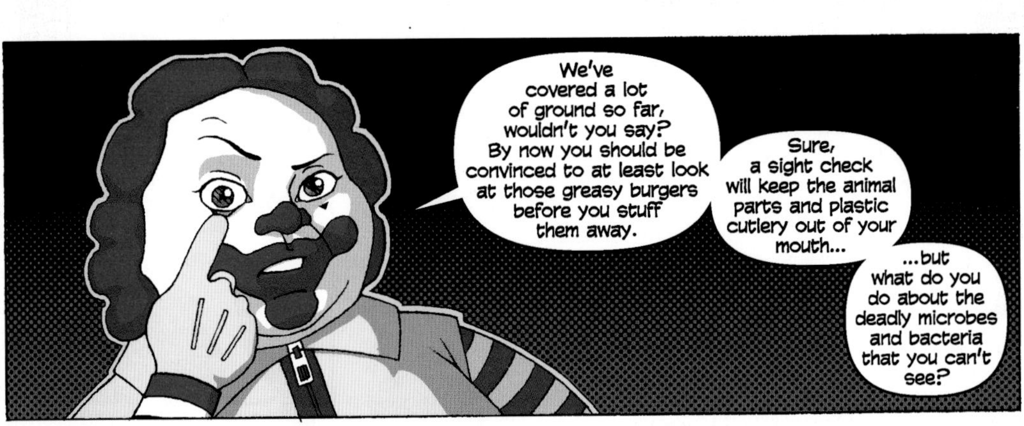
We've covered a lot of ground so far, wouldn't you say? By now you should be convinced to at least look at those greasy burgers before you stuff them away.
Sure, a sight check will keep the animal parts and plastic cutlery out of your mouth...
...but what do you do about the deadly microbes and bacteria that you can't see?

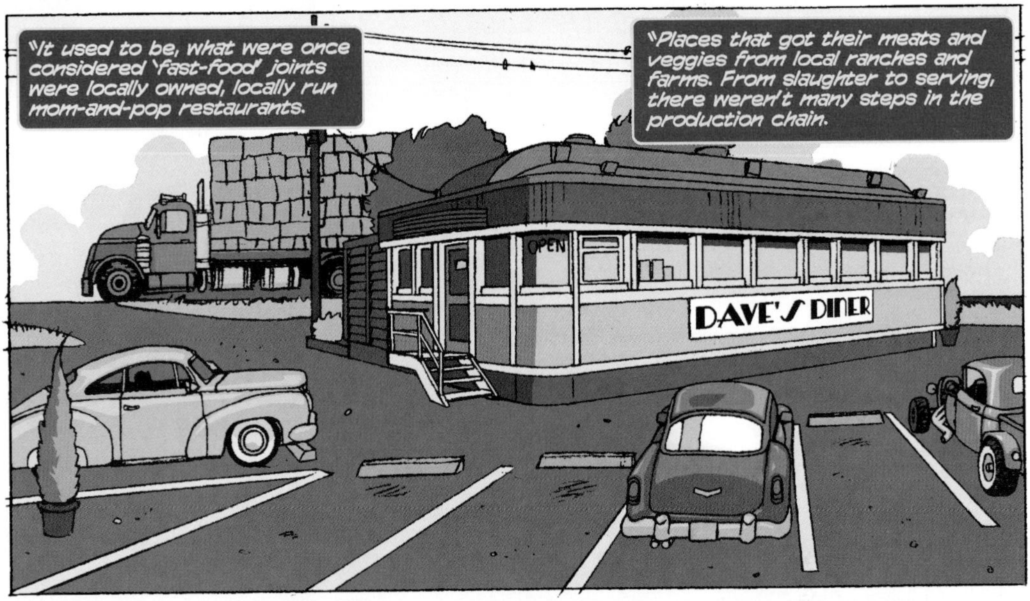
"It used to be, what were once considered 'fast-food' joints were locally owned, locally run mom-and-pop restaurants.
"Places that got their meats and veggies from local ranches and farms. From slaughter to serving, there weren't many steps in the production chain.
OPEN
DAVE'S DINER

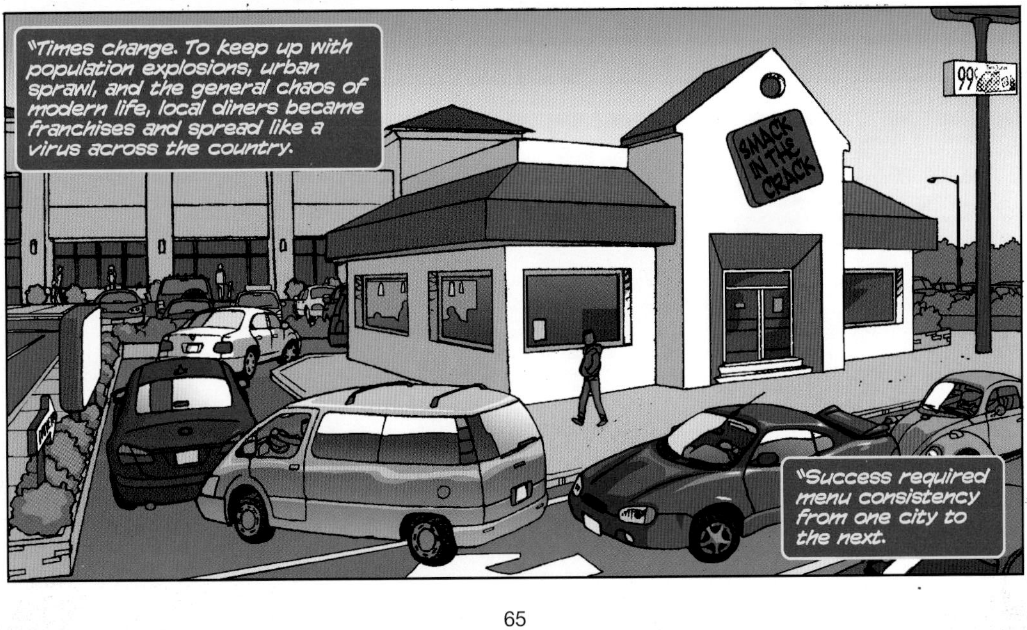
"Times change. To keep up with population explosions, urban sprawl, and the general chaos of modern life, local diners became franchises and spread like a virus across the country.
99¢
SMACK IN THE CRACK
"Success required menu consistency from one city to the next.

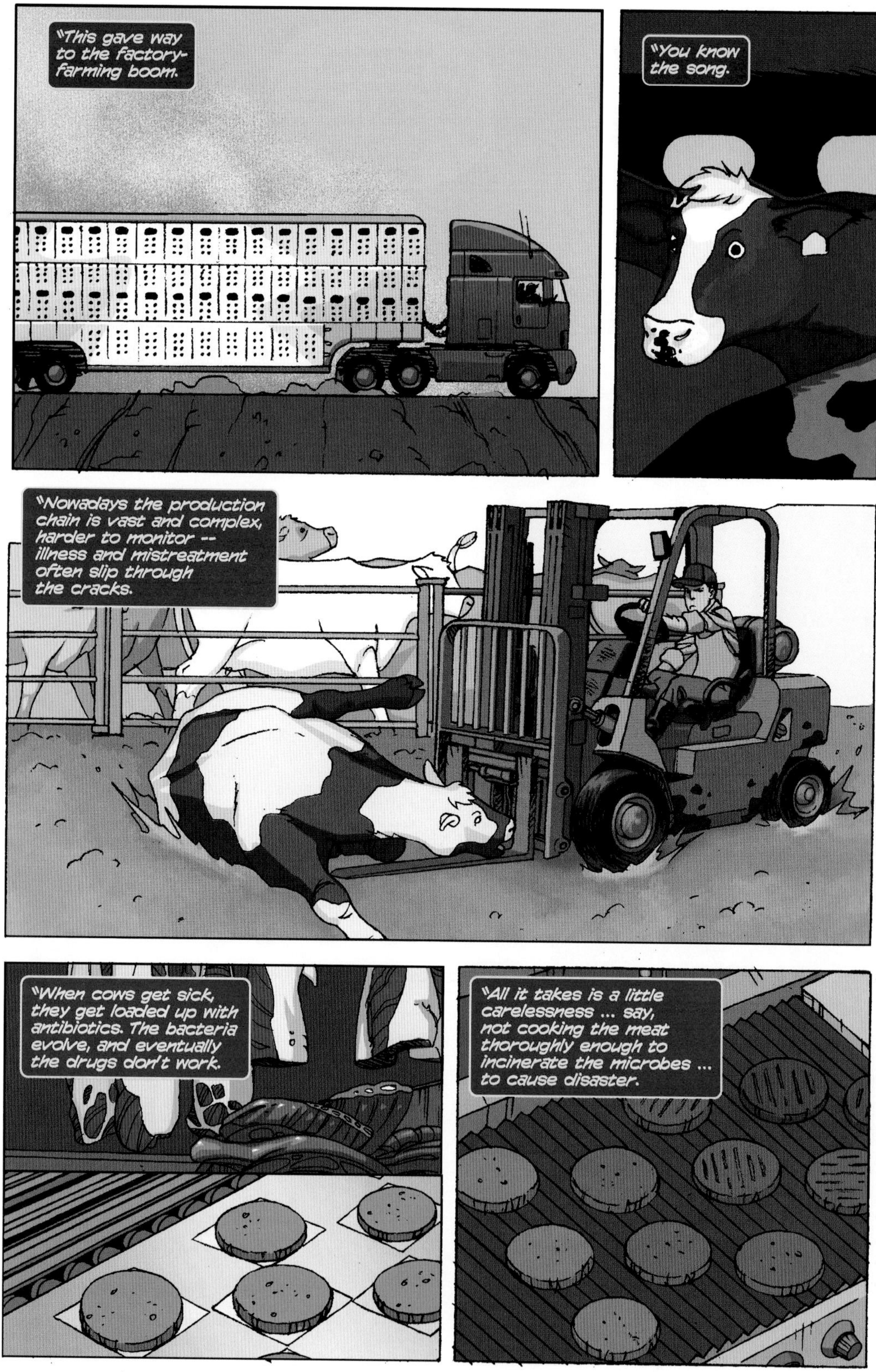
"This gave way to the factory-farming boom.
"You know the song.
"Nowadays the production chain is vast and complex, harder to monitor -- illness and mistreatment often slip through the cracks.
"When cows get sick, they get loaded up with antibiotics. The bacteria evolve, and eventually the drugs don't work.
"All it takes is a little carelessness ... say, not cooking the meat thoroughly enough to incinerate the microbes ... to cause disaster.

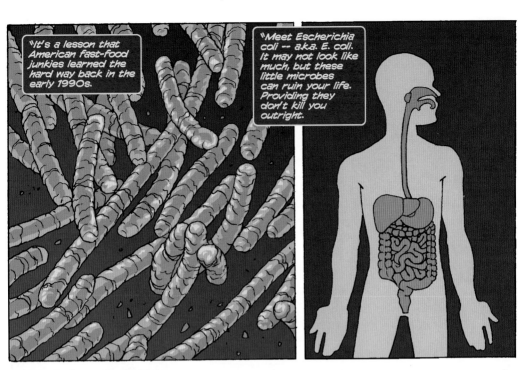

"It's a lesson that American fast-food junkies learned the hard way back in the early 1990s.

"Meet Escherichia coli -- a.k.a. E. coli. It may not look like much, but these little microbes can ruin your life. Providing they don't kill you outright.

"Now, E. coli comes in several different strains -- and most are commonly found in our lower intestine. These are harmless.

"The strain you gotta watch out for is O157:H7 -- which lives in the digestive systems and fecal matter of cows.

"To meet demand, industrial meat packers grind up all kinds of low-grade material into the beef...

"...that's right -- trace amounts of cow crap gets in there, too.

"After eating one of the tainted burgers, Brianne was hit with H.U.S. -- hemolytic uremic syndrome. Her symptoms started almost immediately -- stomach cramping, bloody diarrhea...

"A few days later the toxin produced by the E. coli bacteria attacked her brain, liver, and kidneys. Her pancreas shut down.

"She suffered seizures and strokes and eventually fell into a coma.

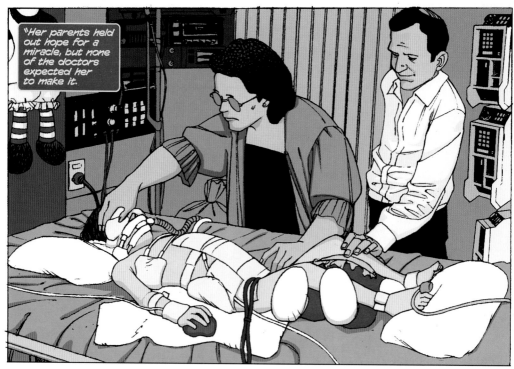

"Her parents held out hope for a miracle, but none of the doctors expected her to make it.

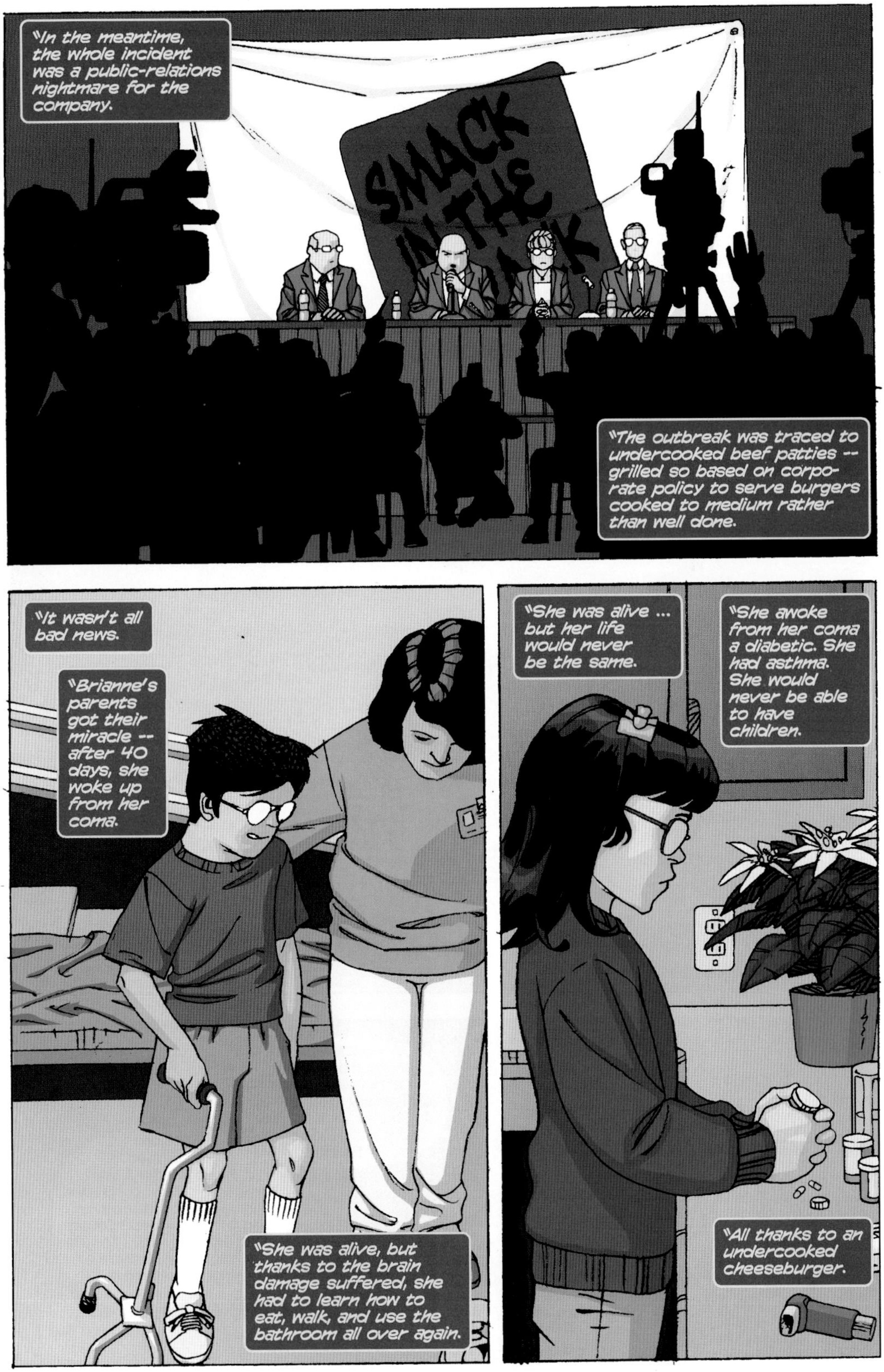
"In the meantime, the whole incident was a public-relations nightmare for the company.
SMACK IN THE
"The outbreak was traced to undercooked beef patties -- grilled so based on corporate policy to serve burgers cooked to medium rather than well done.
"It wasn't all bad news.
"Brianne's parents got their miracle -- after 40 days, she woke up from her coma.
"She was alive, but thanks to the brain damage suffered, she had to learn how to eat, walk, and use the bathroom all over again.
"She was alive ... but her life would never be the same.
"She awoke from her coma a diabetic. She had asthma. She would never be able to have children.
"All thanks to an undercooked cheeseburger.

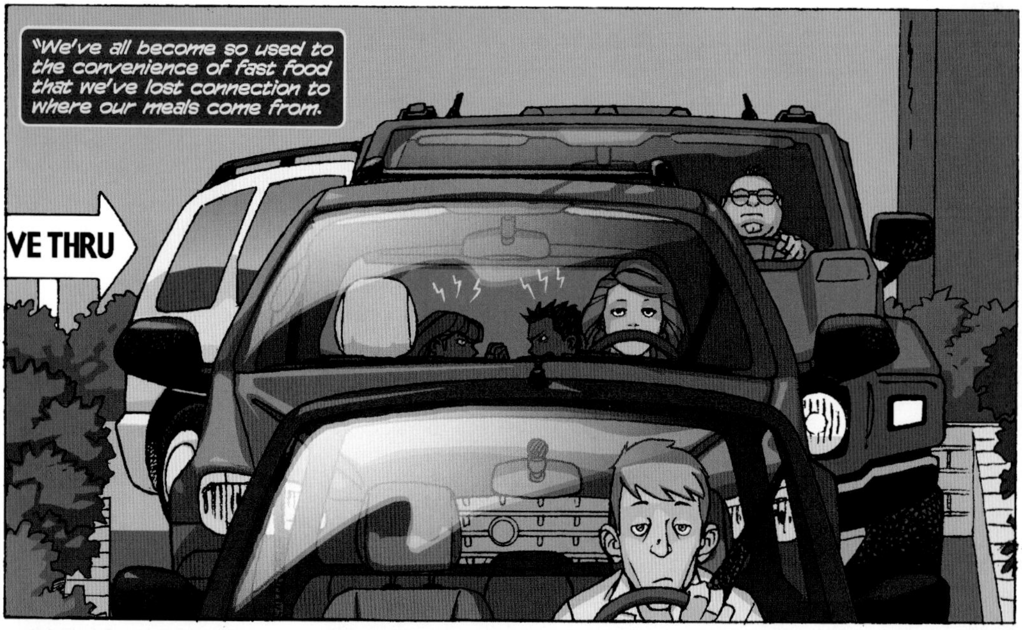

"We've all become so used to the convenience of fast food that we've lost connection to where our meals come from.
VE THRU

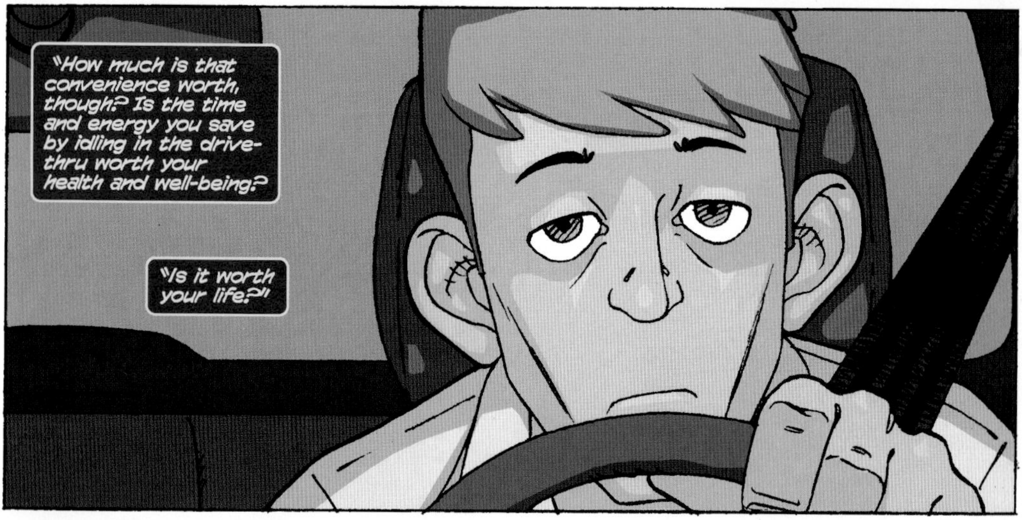

"How much is that convenience worth, though? Is the time and energy you save by idling in the drive-thru worth your health and well-being?
"Is it worth your life?"

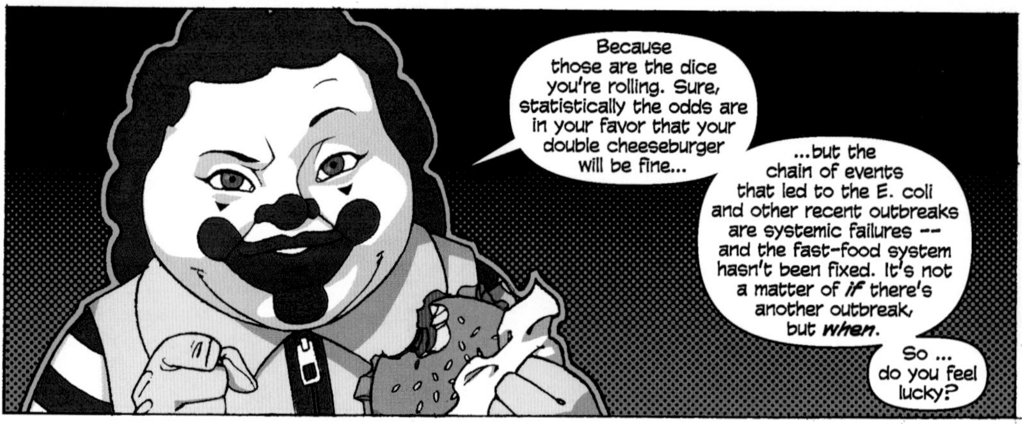

Because those are the dice you're rolling. Sure, statistically the odds are in your favor that your double cheeseburger will be fine...
...but the chain of events that led to the E. coli and other recent outbreaks are systemic failures -- and the fast-food system hasn't been fixed. It's not a matter of *if* there's another outbreak, but ***when***.
So ... do you feel lucky?

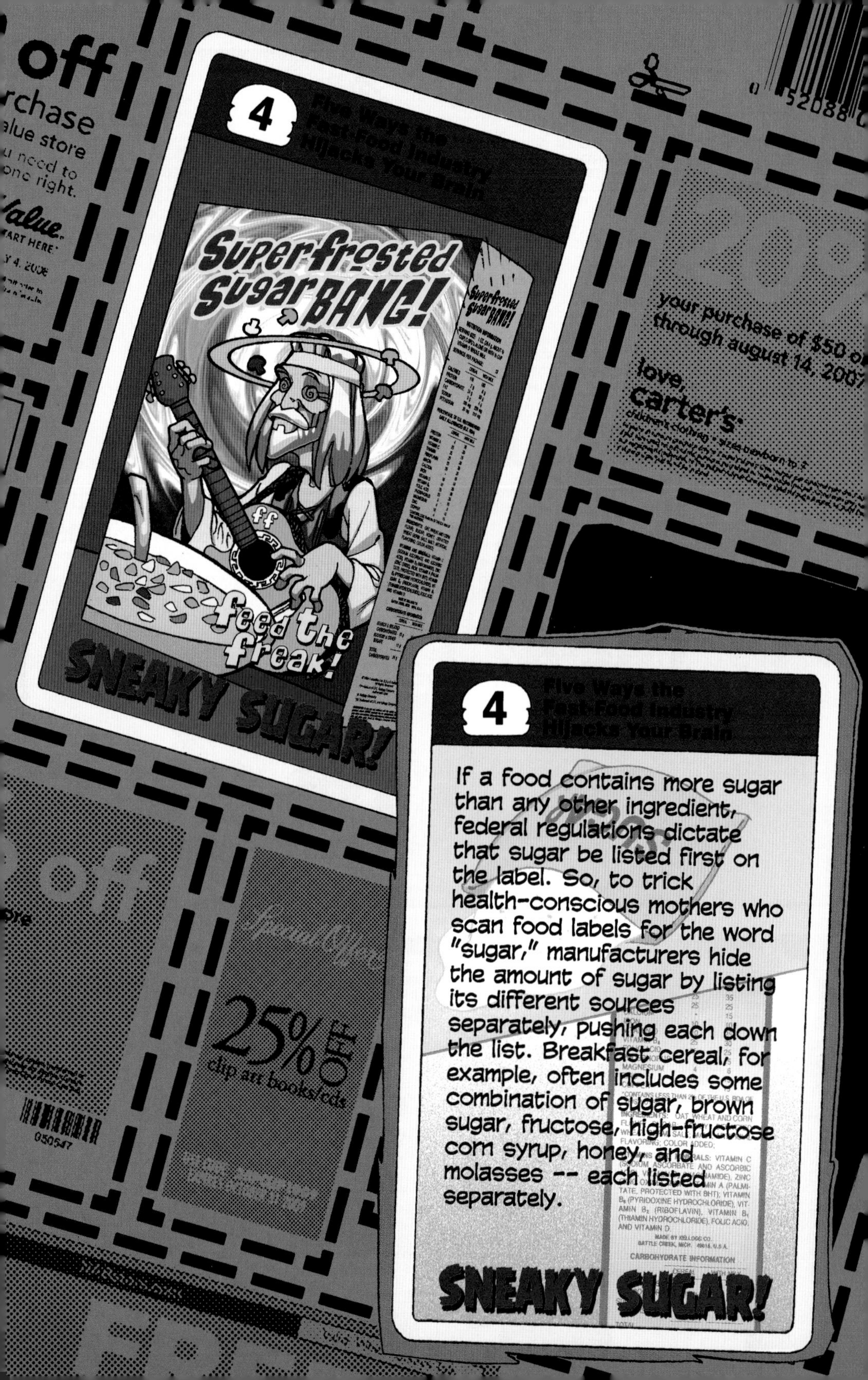
4
Five Ways the Fast-Food Industry Hijacks Your Brain
Superfrosted Sugar BANG!
feed the freak!
SNEAKY SUGAR!
4
Five Ways the Fast-Food Industry Hijacks Your Brain
If a food contains more sugar than any other ingredient, federal regulations dictate that sugar be listed first on the label. So, to trick health-conscious mothers who scan food labels for the word "sugar," manufacturers hide the amount of sugar by listing its different sources separately, pushing each down the list. Breakfast cereal, for example, often includes some combination of sugar, brown sugar, fructose, high-fructose corn syrup, honey, and molasses -- each listed separately.
SNEAKY SUGAR!
off
rchase
your purchase of $50 o
through august 14, 2007
love,
carter's
25% OFF
clip art books/cds

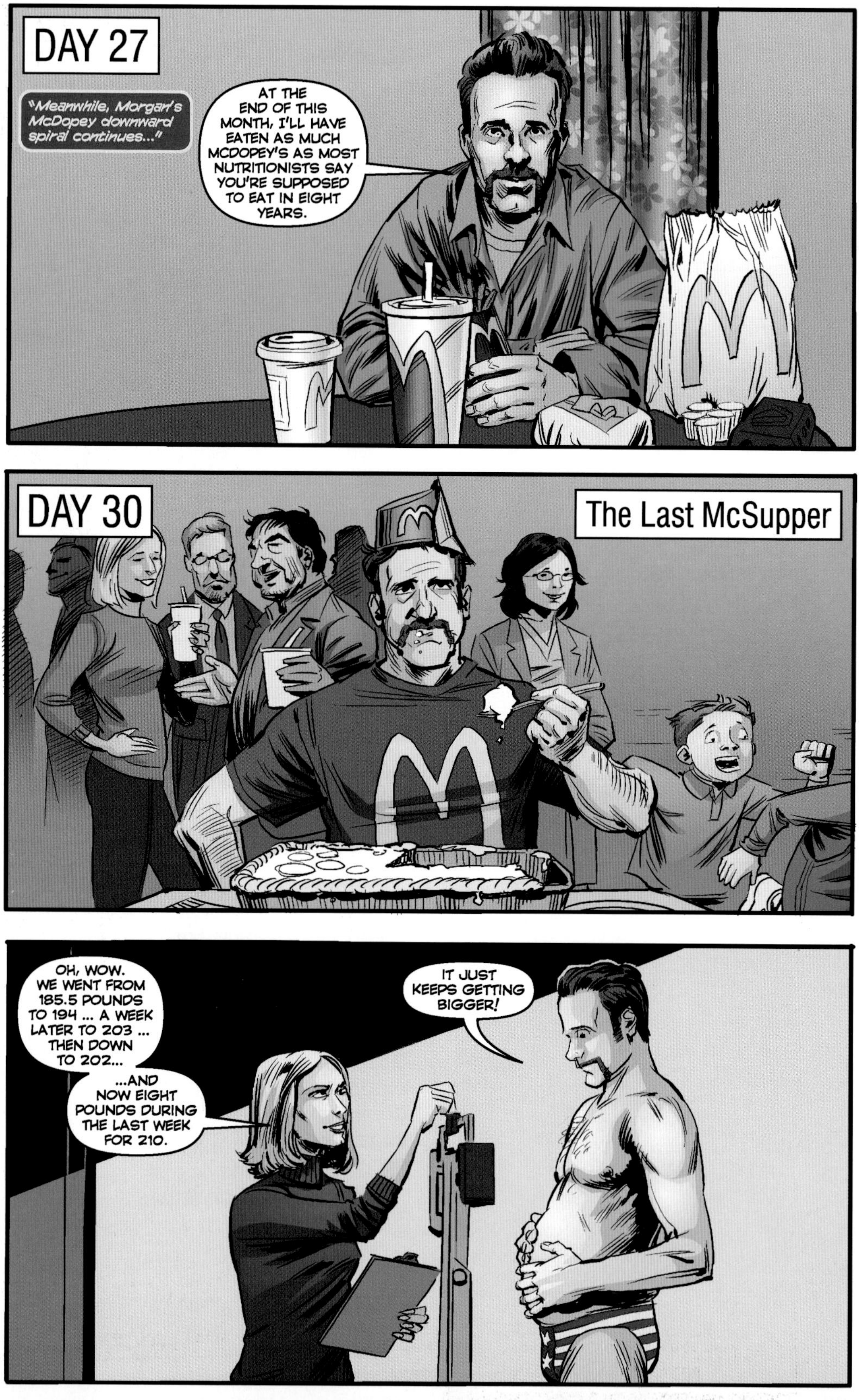
DAY 27
"Meanwhile, Morgan's McDopey downward spiral continues..."
AT THE END OF THIS MONTH, I'LL HAVE EATEN AS MUCH MCDOPEY'S AS MOST NUTRITIONISTS SAY YOU'RE SUPPOSED TO EAT IN EIGHT YEARS.
DAY 30
The Last McSupper
OH, WOW. WE WENT FROM 185.5 POUNDS TO 194 ... A WEEK LATER TO 203 ... THEN DOWN TO 202...
IT JUST KEEPS GETTING BIGGER!
...AND NOW EIGHT POUNDS DURING THE LAST WEEK FOR 210.

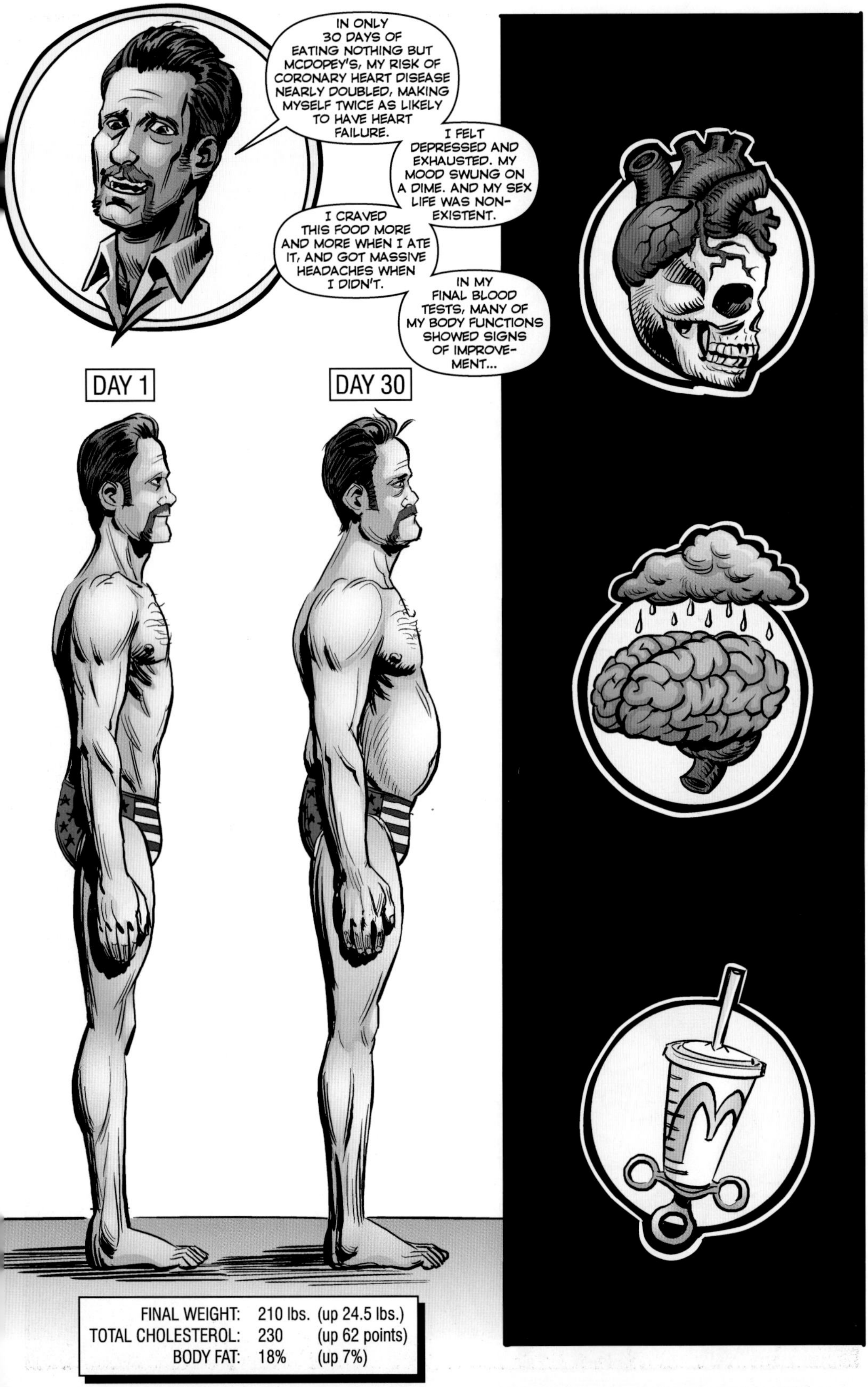

IN ONLY 30 DAYS OF EATING NOTHING BUT MCDOPEY'S, MY RISK OF CORONARY HEART DISEASE NEARLY DOUBLED, MAKING MYSELF TWICE AS LIKELY TO HAVE HEART FAILURE.
I FELT DEPRESSED AND EXHAUSTED. MY MOOD SWUNG ON A DIME. AND MY SEX LIFE WAS NON-EXISTENT.
I CRAVED THIS FOOD MORE AND MORE WHEN I ATE IT, AND GOT MASSIVE HEADACHES WHEN I DIDN'T.
IN MY FINAL BLOOD TESTS, MANY OF MY BODY FUNCTIONS SHOWED SIGNS OF IMPROVE-MENT...
DAY 1
DAY 30
FINAL WEIGHT: 210 lbs. (up 24.5 lbs.)
TOTAL CHOLESTEROL: 230 (up 62 points)
BODY FAT: 18% (up 7%)

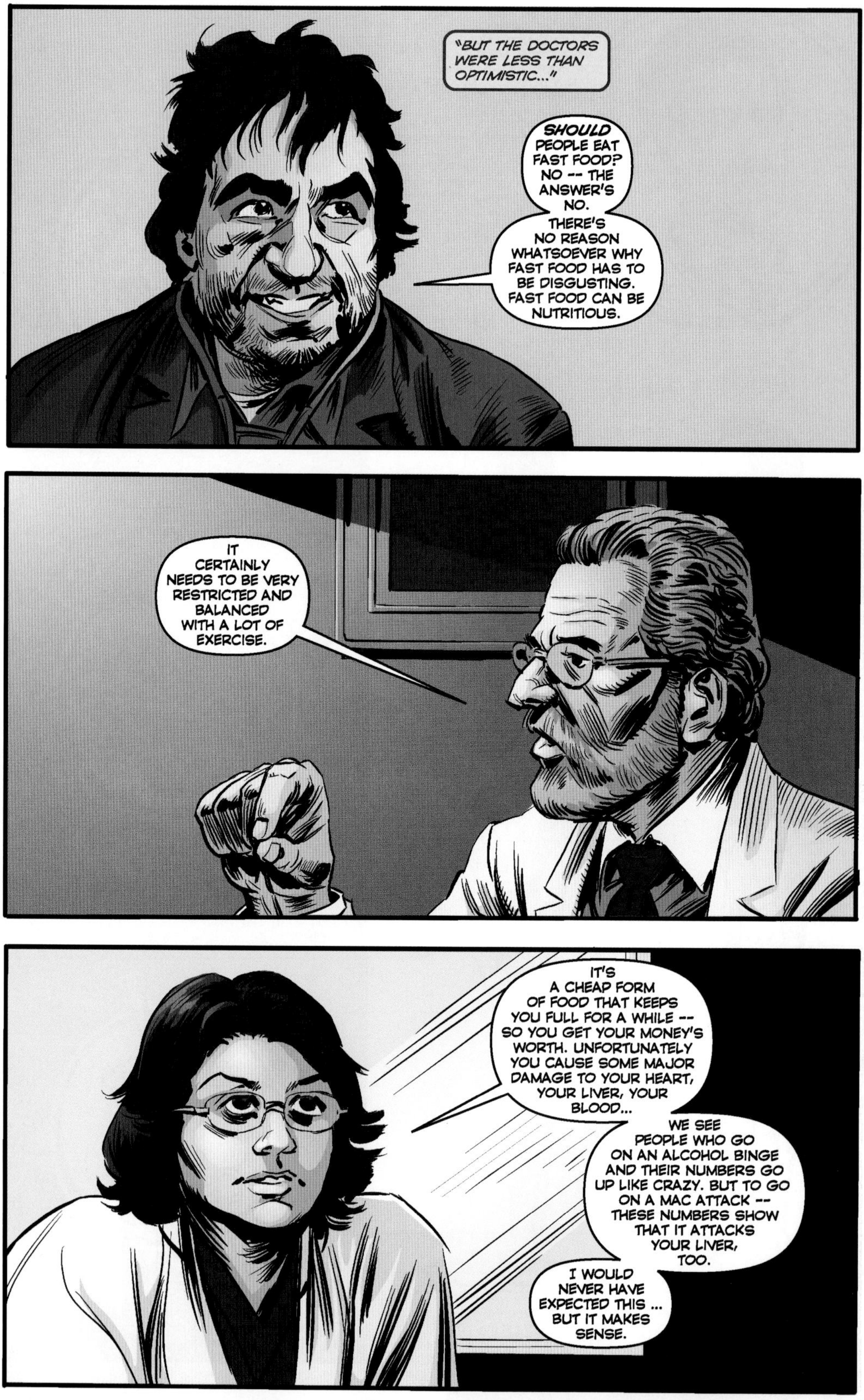
"BUT THE DOCTORS WERE LESS THAN OPTIMISTIC..."
SHOULD PEOPLE EAT FAST FOOD? NO -- THE ANSWER'S NO.
THERE'S NO REASON WHATSOEVER WHY FAST FOOD HAS TO BE DISGUSTING. FAST FOOD CAN BE NUTRITIOUS.
IT CERTAINLY NEEDS TO BE VERY RESTRICTED AND BALANCED WITH A LOT OF EXERCISE.
IT'S A CHEAP FORM OF FOOD THAT KEEPS YOU FULL FOR A WHILE -- SO YOU GET YOUR MONEY'S WORTH. UNFORTUNATELY YOU CAUSE SOME MAJOR DAMAGE TO YOUR HEART, YOUR LIVER, YOUR BLOOD...
WE SEE PEOPLE WHO GO ON AN ALCOHOL BINGE AND THEIR NUMBERS GO UP LIKE CRAZY. BUT TO GO ON A MAC ATTACK -- THESE NUMBERS SHOW THAT IT ATTACKS YOUR LIVER, TOO.
I WOULD NEVER HAVE EXPECTED THIS ... BUT IT MAKES SENSE.

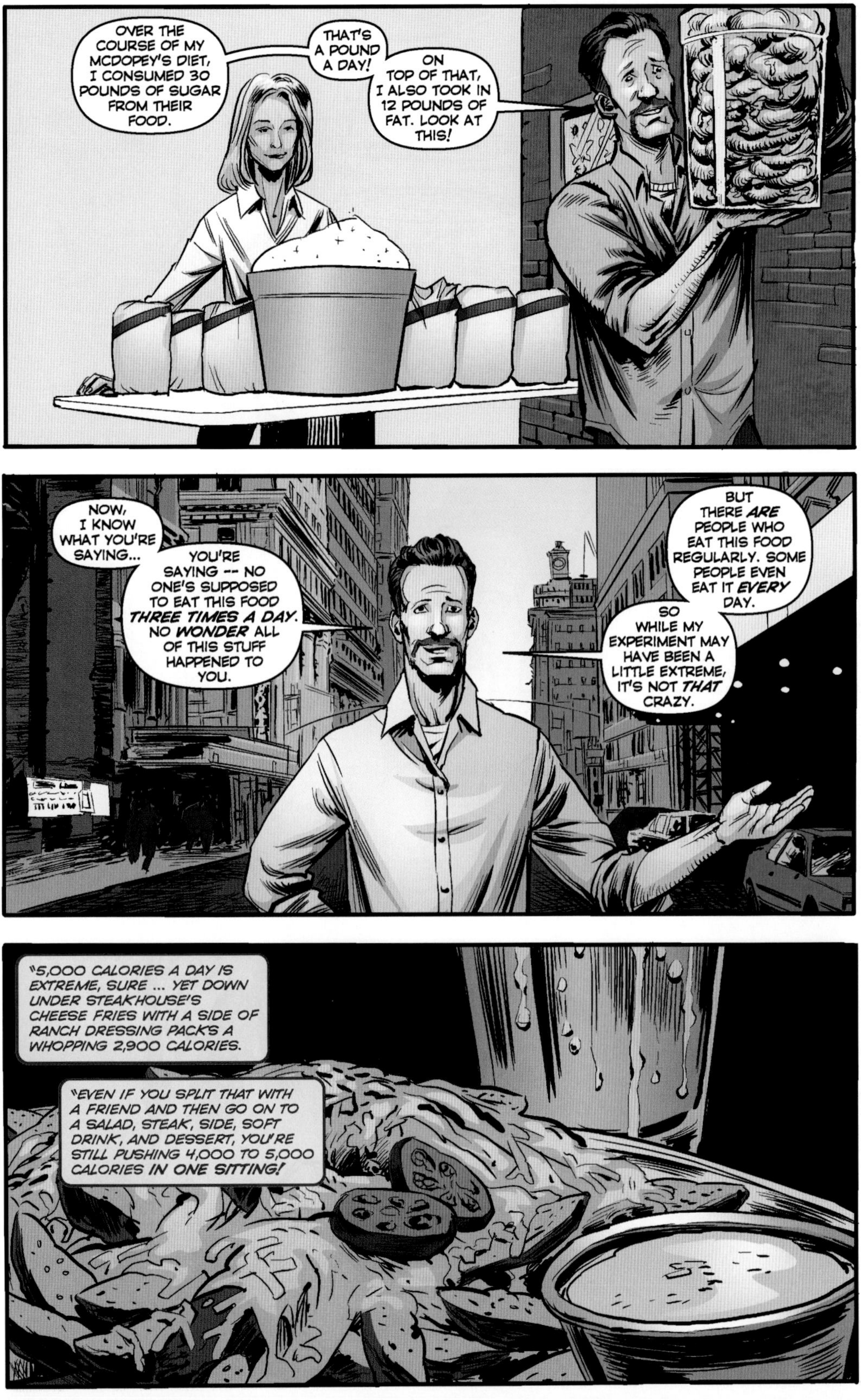

OVER THE COURSE OF MY MCDOPEY'S DIET, I CONSUMED 30 POUNDS OF SUGAR FROM THEIR FOOD.
THAT'S A POUND A DAY!
ON TOP OF THAT, I ALSO TOOK IN 12 POUNDS OF FAT. LOOK AT THIS!
NOW, I KNOW WHAT YOU'RE SAYING...
YOU'RE SAYING -- NO ONE'S SUPPOSED TO EAT THIS FOOD THREE TIMES A DAY. NO WONDER ALL OF THIS STUFF HAPPENED TO YOU.
BUT THERE ARE PEOPLE WHO EAT THIS FOOD REGULARLY. SOME PEOPLE EVEN EAT IT EVERY DAY.
SO WHILE MY EXPERIMENT MAY HAVE BEEN A LITTLE EXTREME, IT'S NOT THAT CRAZY.
"5,000 CALORIES A DAY IS EXTREME, SURE ... YET DOWN UNDER STEAKHOUSE'S CHEESE FRIES WITH A SIDE OF RANCH DRESSING PACKS A WHOPPING 2,900 CALORIES.
"EVEN IF YOU SPLIT THAT WITH A FRIEND AND THEN GO ON TO A SALAD, STEAK, SIDE, SOFT DRINK, AND DESSERT, YOU'RE STILL PUSHING 4,000 TO 5,000 CALORIES IN ONE SITTING!

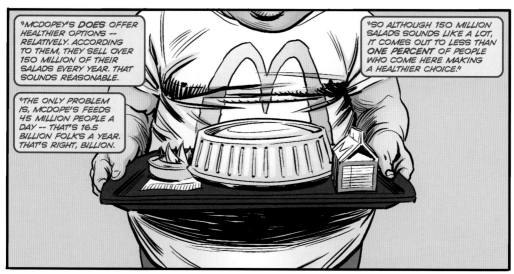

"MCDOPEY'S *DOES* OFFER HEALTHIER OPTIONS -- RELATIVELY. ACCORDING TO THEM, THEY SELL OVER 150 MILLION OF THEIR SALADS EVERY YEAR. THAT SOUNDS REASONABLE.

"THE ONLY PROBLEM IS, MCDOPE'S FEEDS 45 MILLION PEOPLE A DAY -- THAT'S 16.5 BILLION FOLKS A YEAR. THAT'S RIGHT, BILLION."

"SO ALTHOUGH 150 MILLION SALADS SOUNDS LIKE A LOT, IT COMES OUT TO LESS THAN *ONE PERCENT* OF PEOPLE WHO COME HERE MAKING A HEALTHIER CHOICE."

IF YOU EAT HERE ONCE OR TWICE A WEEK -- JUST LIKE THE ROUGHLY 72% OF MCDOPEY'S CUSTOMERS THAT DO -- THEN YOU ARE WHAT THE COMPANY CALLS ONE OF THEIR "HEAVY USERS."

EAT THIS STUFF THREE OR *MORE* TIMES A WEEK, THOUGH, AND YOU MOVE INTO "SUPER HEAVY USER" TERRITORY...

...JOINING THE ALMOST *TEN MILLION* PEOPLE WHO MAKE UP THE OTHER 22% OF MCDOPEY'S CUSTOMERS.

WHICH KIND OF "USER" ARE YOU?

WHICH KIND DO YOU WANT TO BE?

Chill

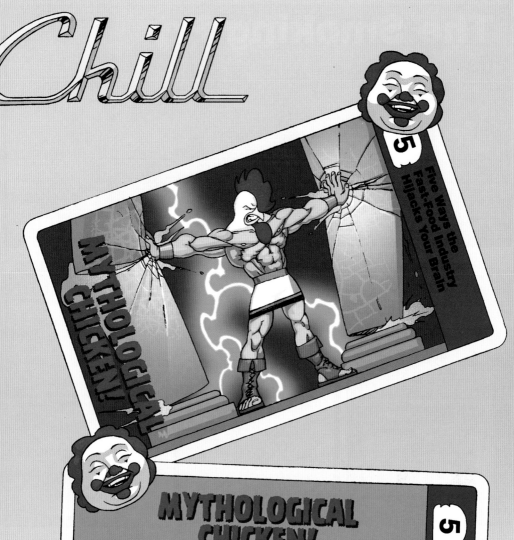

5

Five Ways the Fast-Food Industry Hijacks Your Brain

MYTHOLOGICAL CHICKEN!

THE MYTH OF HEALTHY GRILLED CHICKEN

Think you're eating healthy when you order the grilled, marinated chicken? Think again.

A common way to get marinade into meat is through needle injection. Hundreds of needles are used to pierce the meat, tearing up the connective tissue, to add solutions of salt, sugar, and fat. These injections not only increase flavor, but they also make the meat fall apart in our mouths.

5

Five Ways the Fast-Food Industry Hijacks Your Brain

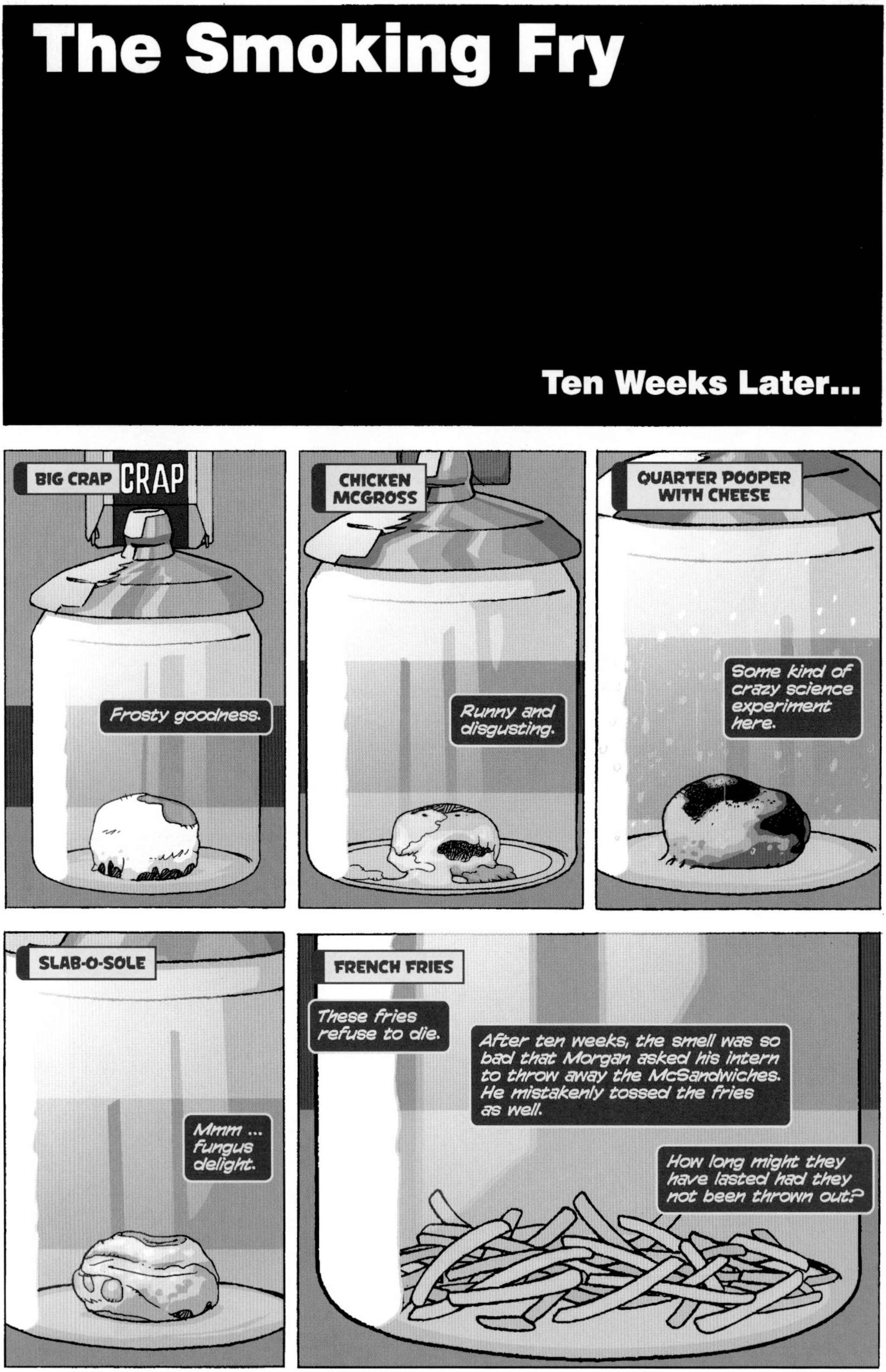
The Smoking Fry
Ten Weeks Later...
BIG CRAP
CRAP
Frosty goodness.
CHICKEN MCGROSS
Runny and disgusting.
QUARTER POOPER WITH CHEESE
Some kind of crazy science experiment here.
SLAB-O-SOLE
Mmm ... fungus delight.
FRENCH FRIES
These fries refuse to die.
After ten weeks, the smell was so bad that Morgan asked his intern to throw away the McSandwiches. He mistakenly tossed the fries as well.
How long might they have lasted had they not been thrown out?

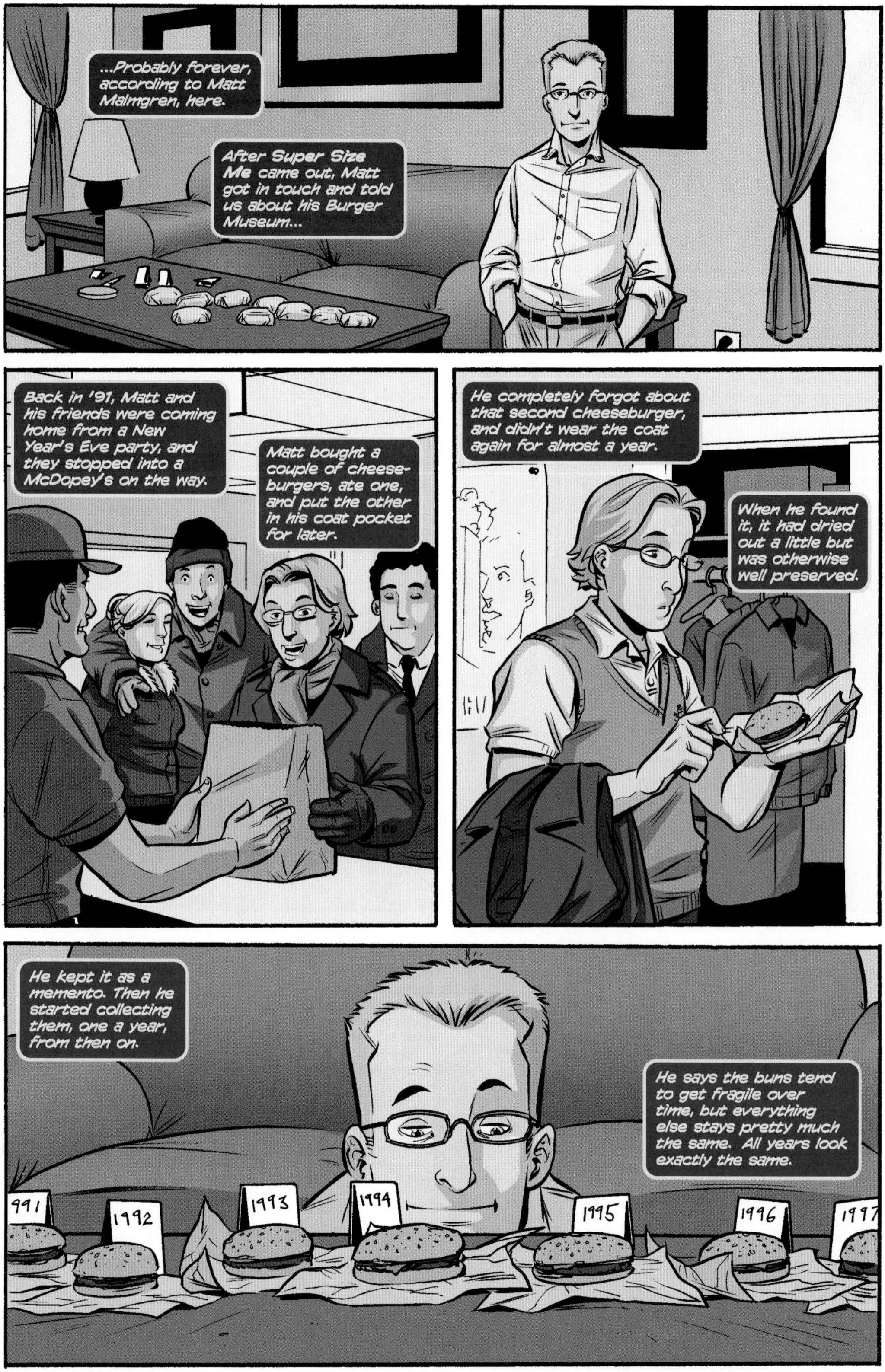
...Probably forever, according to Matt Malmgren, here.
After Super Size Me came out, Matt got in touch and told us about his Burger Museum...
Back in '91, Matt and his friends were coming home from a New Year's Eve party, and they stopped into a McDopey's on the way.
Matt bought a couple of cheese-burgers, ate one, and put the other in his coat pocket for later.
He completely forgot about that second cheeseburger, and didn't wear the coat again for almost a year.
When he found it, it had dried out a little but was otherwise well preserved.
He kept it as a memento. Then he started collecting them, one a year, from then on.
He says the buns tend to get fragile over time, but everything else stays pretty much the same. All years look exactly the same.
991
1992
1993
1994
1995
1996
1997

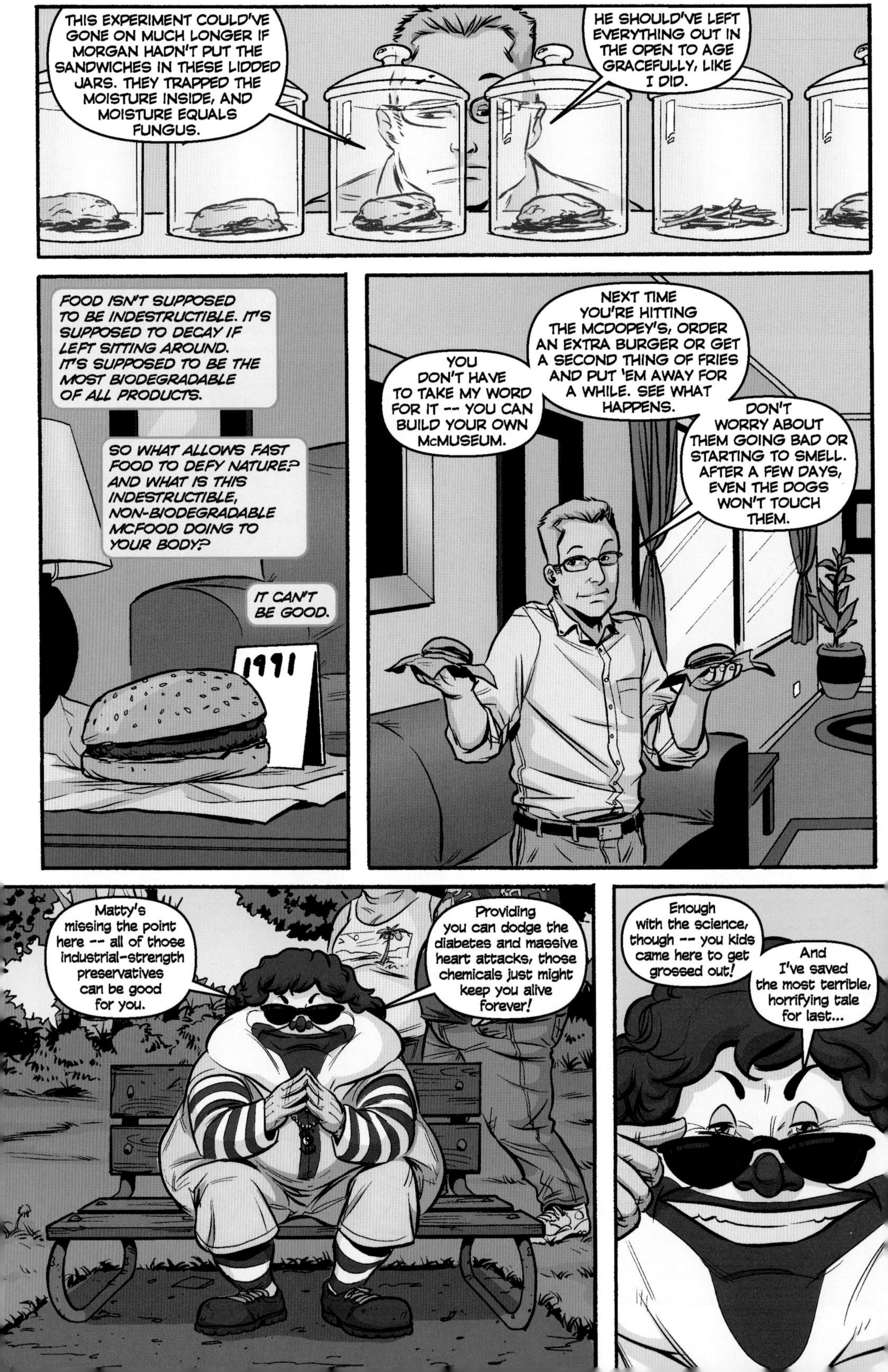
THIS EXPERIMENT COULD'VE GONE ON MUCH LONGER IF MORGAN HADN'T PUT THE SANDWICHES IN THESE LIDDED JARS. THEY TRAPPED THE MOISTURE INSIDE, AND MOISTURE EQUALS FUNGUS.
HE SHOULD'VE LEFT EVERYTHING OUT IN THE OPEN TO AGE GRACEFULLY, LIKE I DID.
FOOD ISN'T SUPPOSED TO BE INDESTRUCTIBLE. IT'S SUPPOSED TO DECAY IF LEFT SITTING AROUND. IT'S SUPPOSED TO BE THE MOST BIODEGRADABLE OF ALL PRODUCTS.
SO WHAT ALLOWS FAST FOOD TO DEFY NATURE? AND WHAT IS THIS INDESTRUCTIBLE, NON-BIODEGRADABLE MCFOOD DOING TO YOUR BODY?
IT CAN'T BE GOOD.
1991
YOU DON'T HAVE TO TAKE MY WORD FOR IT -- YOU CAN BUILD YOUR OWN McMUSEUM.
NEXT TIME YOU'RE HITTING THE MCDOPEY'S, ORDER AN EXTRA BURGER OR GET A SECOND THING OF FRIES AND PUT 'EM AWAY FOR A WHILE. SEE WHAT HAPPENS.
DON'T WORRY ABOUT THEM GOING BAD OR STARTING TO SMELL. AFTER A FEW DAYS, EVEN THE DOGS WON'T TOUCH THEM.
Matty's missing the point here -- all of those industrial-strength preservatives can be good for you.
Providing you can dodge the diabetes and massive heart attacks, those chemicals just might keep you alive forever!
Enough with the science, though -- you kids came here to get grossed out!
And I've saved the most terrible, horrifying tale for last...

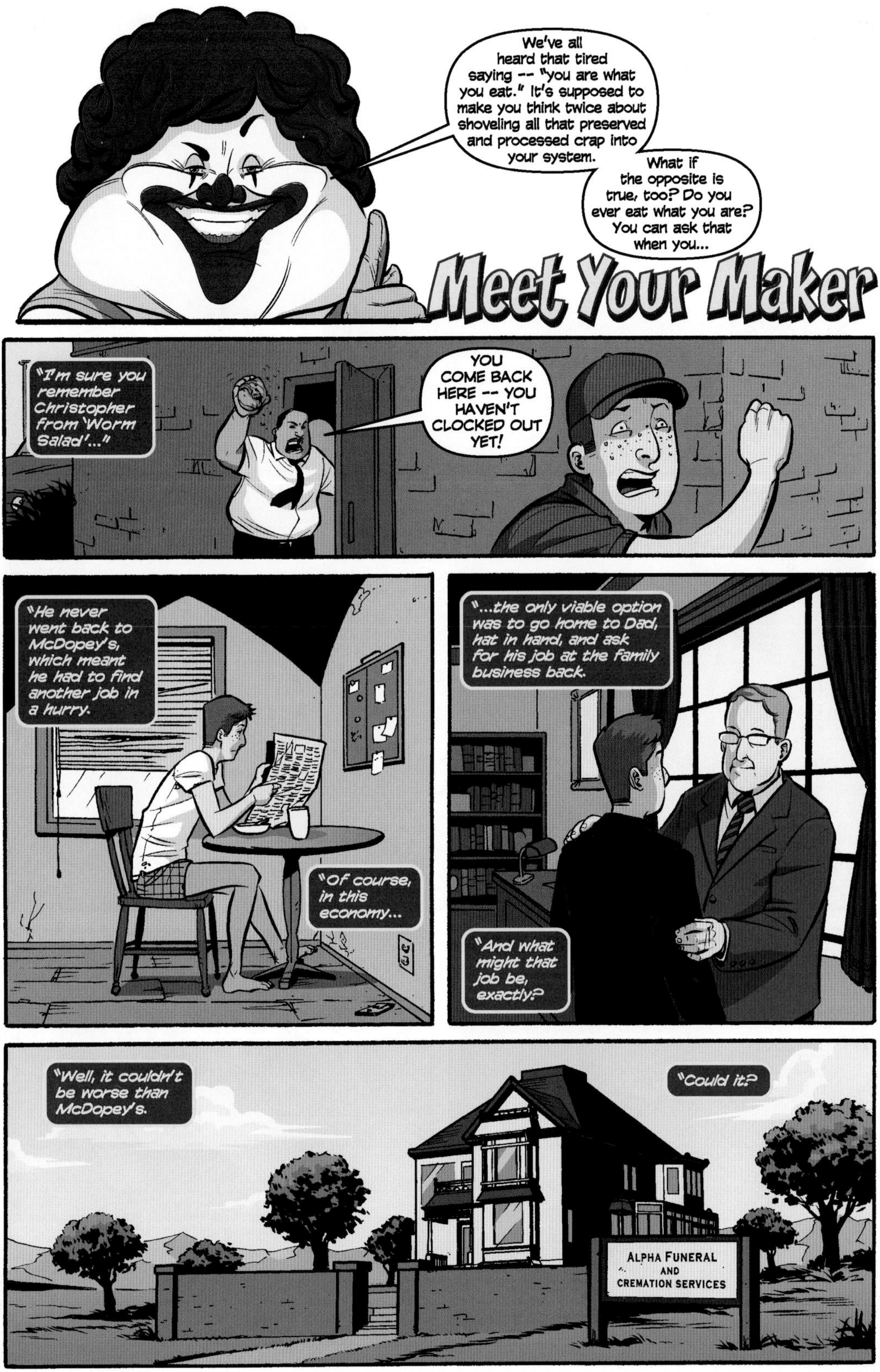
We've all heard that tired saying -- "you are what you eat." It's supposed to make you think twice about shoveling all that preserved and processed crap into your system.
What if the opposite is true, too? Do you ever eat what you are? You can ask that when you...
Meet Your Maker
"I'm sure you remember Christopher from 'Worm Salad'..."
YOU COME BACK HERE -- YOU HAVEN'T CLOCKED OUT YET!
"He never went back to McDopey's, which meant he had to find another job in a hurry.
"Of course, in this economy...
"...the only viable option was to go home to Dad, hat in hand, and ask for his job at the family business back.
"And what might that job be, exactly?
"Well, it couldn't be worse than McDopey's.
"Could it?
ALPHA FUNERAL AND CREMATION SERVICES

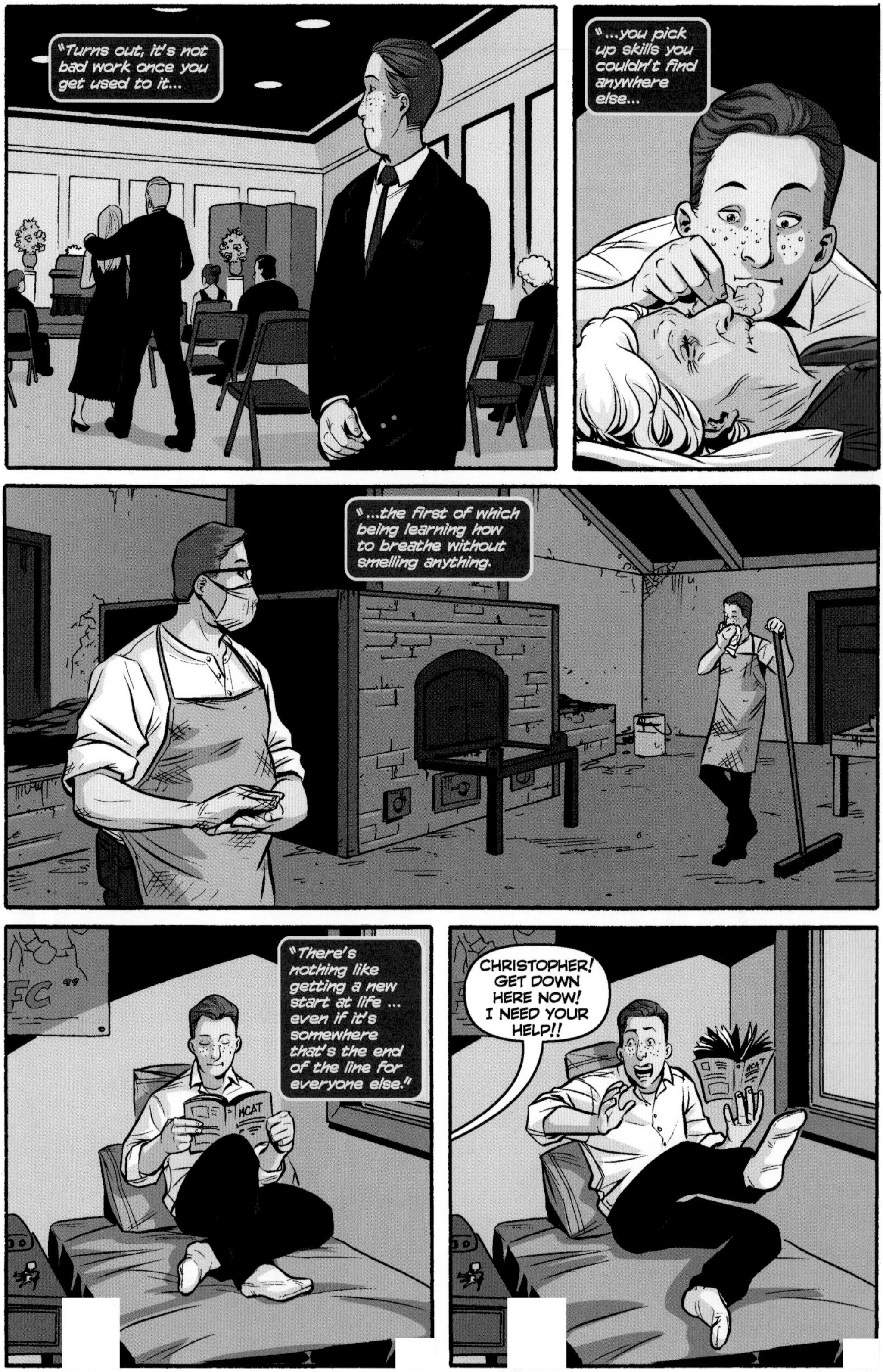
"Turns out, it's not bad work once you get used to it...
"...you pick up skills you couldn't find anywhere else...
"...the first of which being learning how to breathe without smelling anything.
"There's nothing like getting a new start at life ... even if it's somewhere that's the end of the line for everyone else."
MCAT
CHRISTOPHER! GET DOWN HERE NOW! I NEED YOUR HELP!!

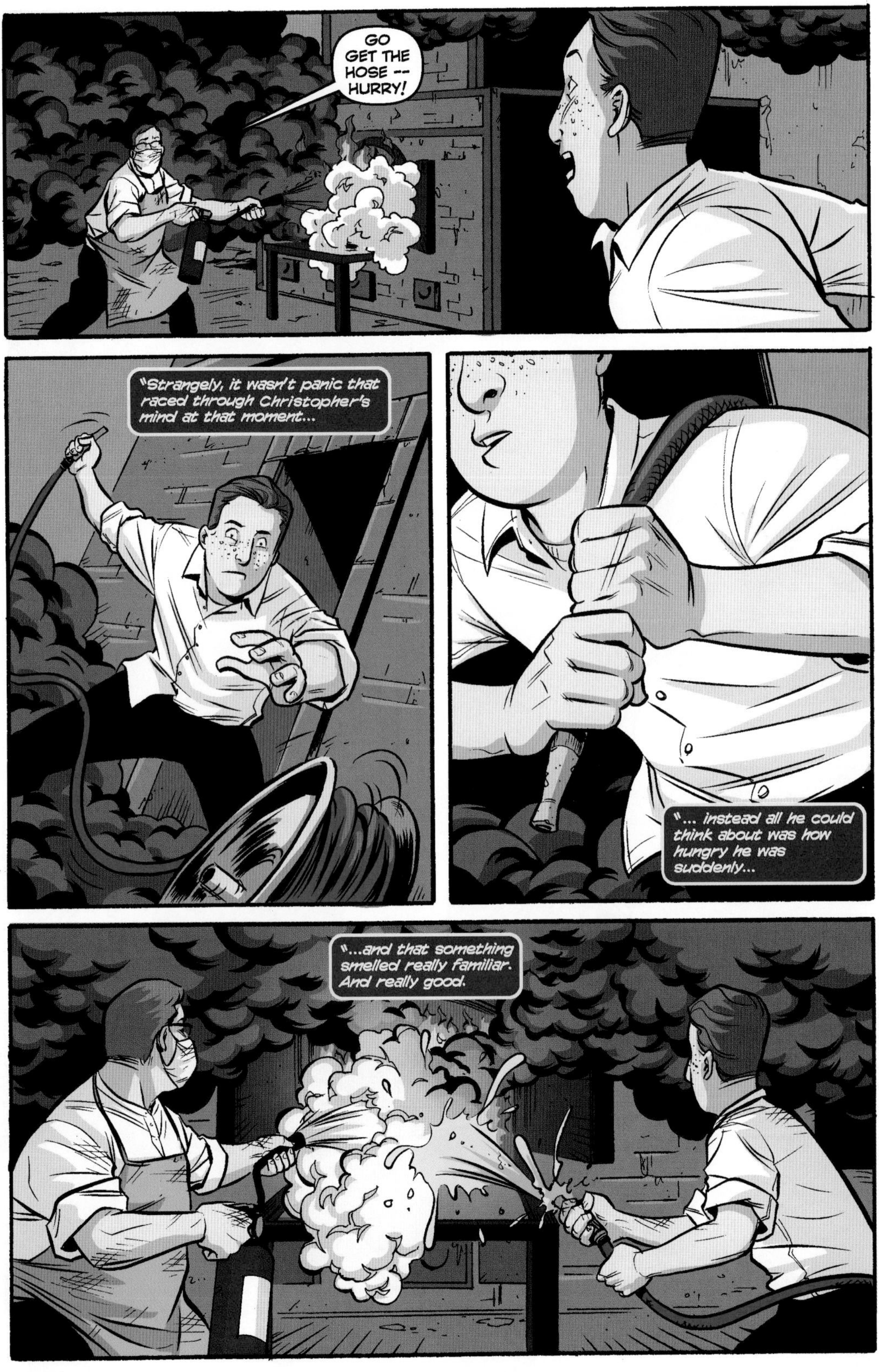
GO GET THE HOSE -- HURRY!
"Strangely, it wasn't panic that raced through Christopher's mind at that moment...
"... instead all he could think about was how hungry he was suddenly...
"...and that something smelled really familiar. And really good.

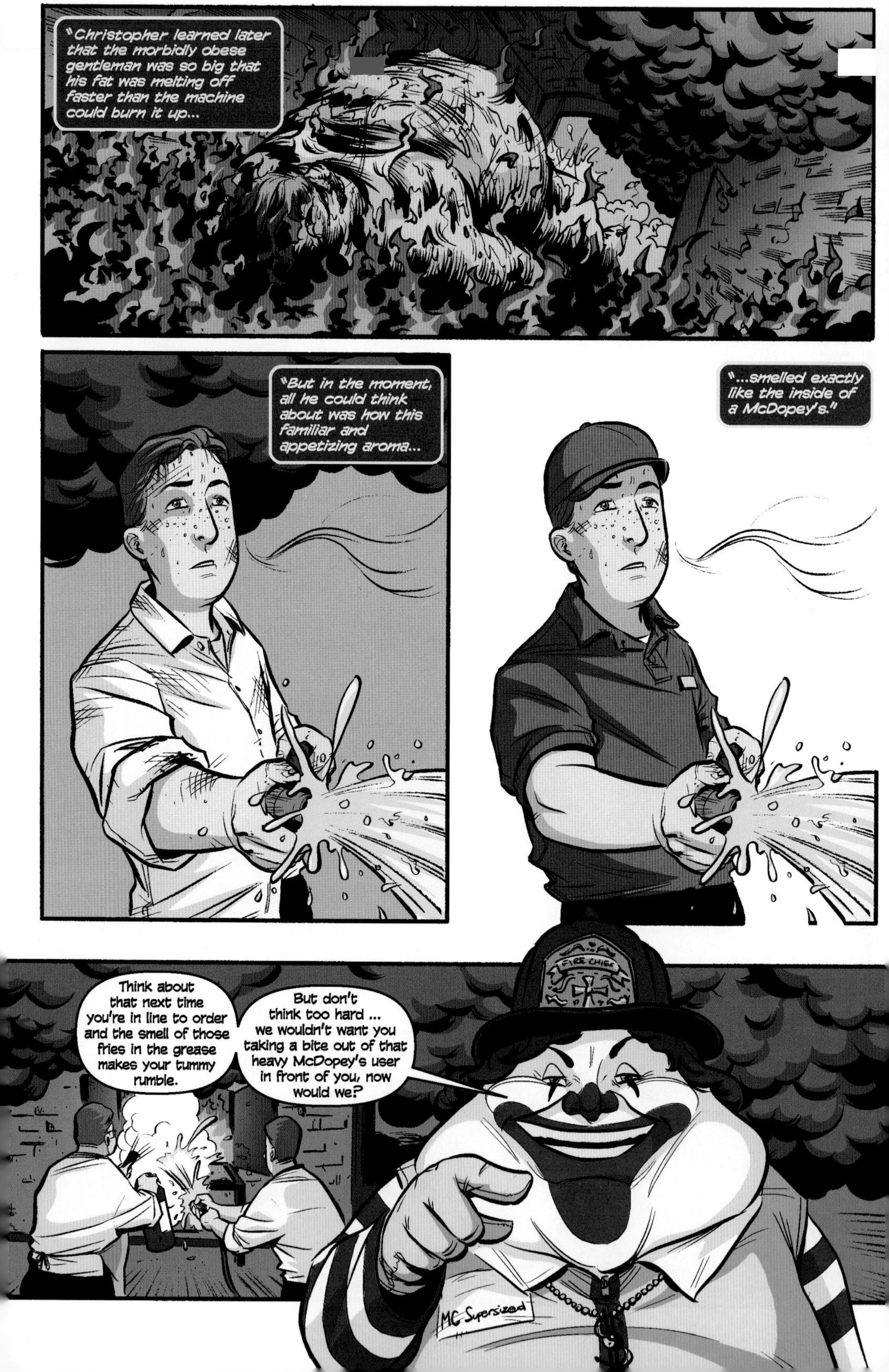

"Christopher learned later that the morbidly obese gentleman was so big that his fat was melting off faster than the machine could burn it up...
"But in the moment, all he could think about was how this familiar and appetizing aroma...
"...smelled exactly like the inside of a McDopey's."
Think about that next time you're in line to order and the smell of those fries in the grease makes your tummy rumble.
But don't think too hard ... we wouldn't want you taking a bite out of that heavy McDopey's user in front of you, now would we?
FIRE CHIEF
MC Supersized

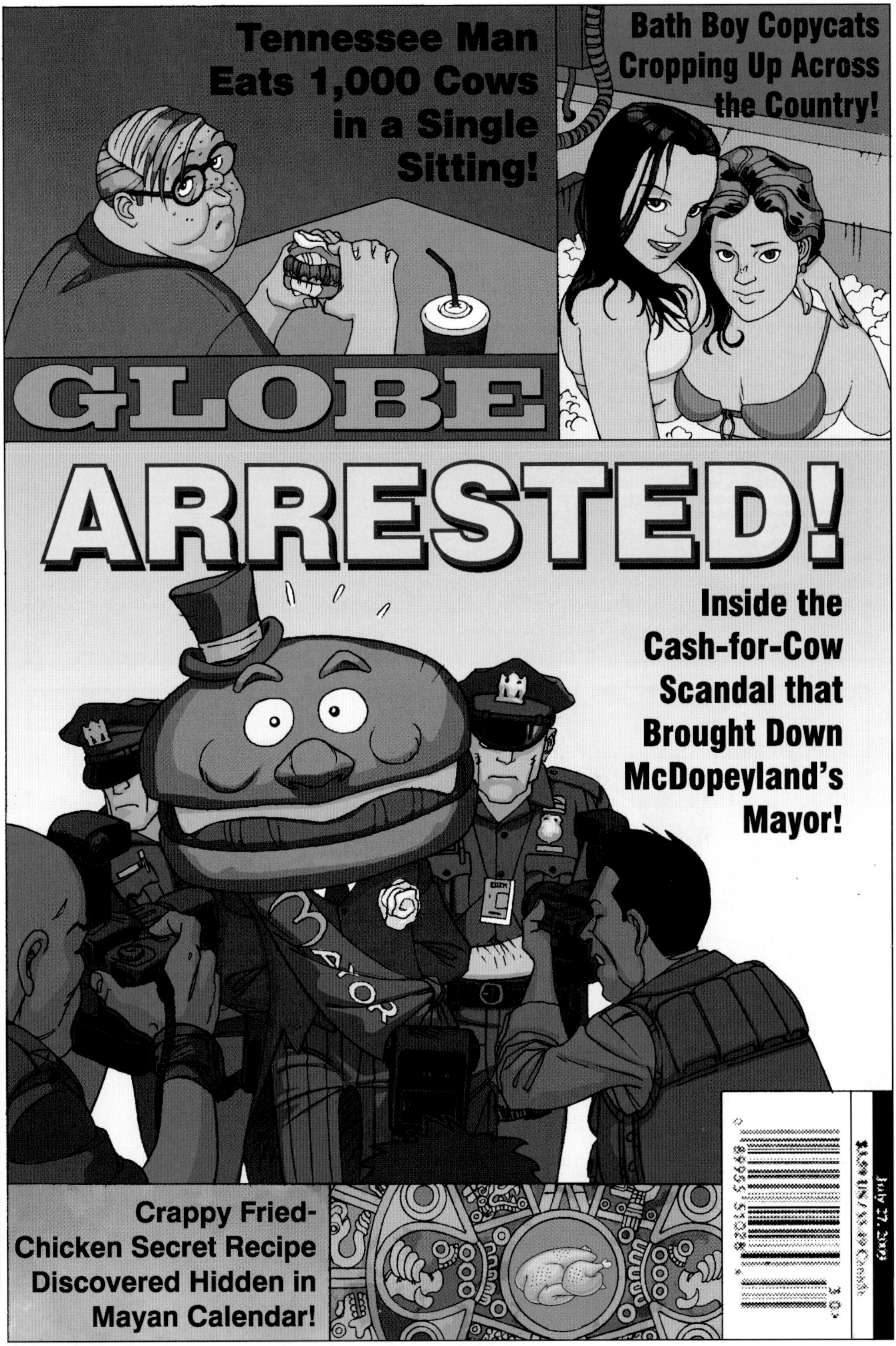
Tennessee Man Eats 1,000 Cows in a Single Sitting!
Bath Boy Copycats Cropping Up Across the Country!
GLOBE
ARRESTED!
Inside the Cash-for-Cow Scandal that Brought Down McDopeyland's Mayor!
MAYOR
Crappy Fried-Chicken Secret Recipe Discovered Hidden in Mayan Calendar!

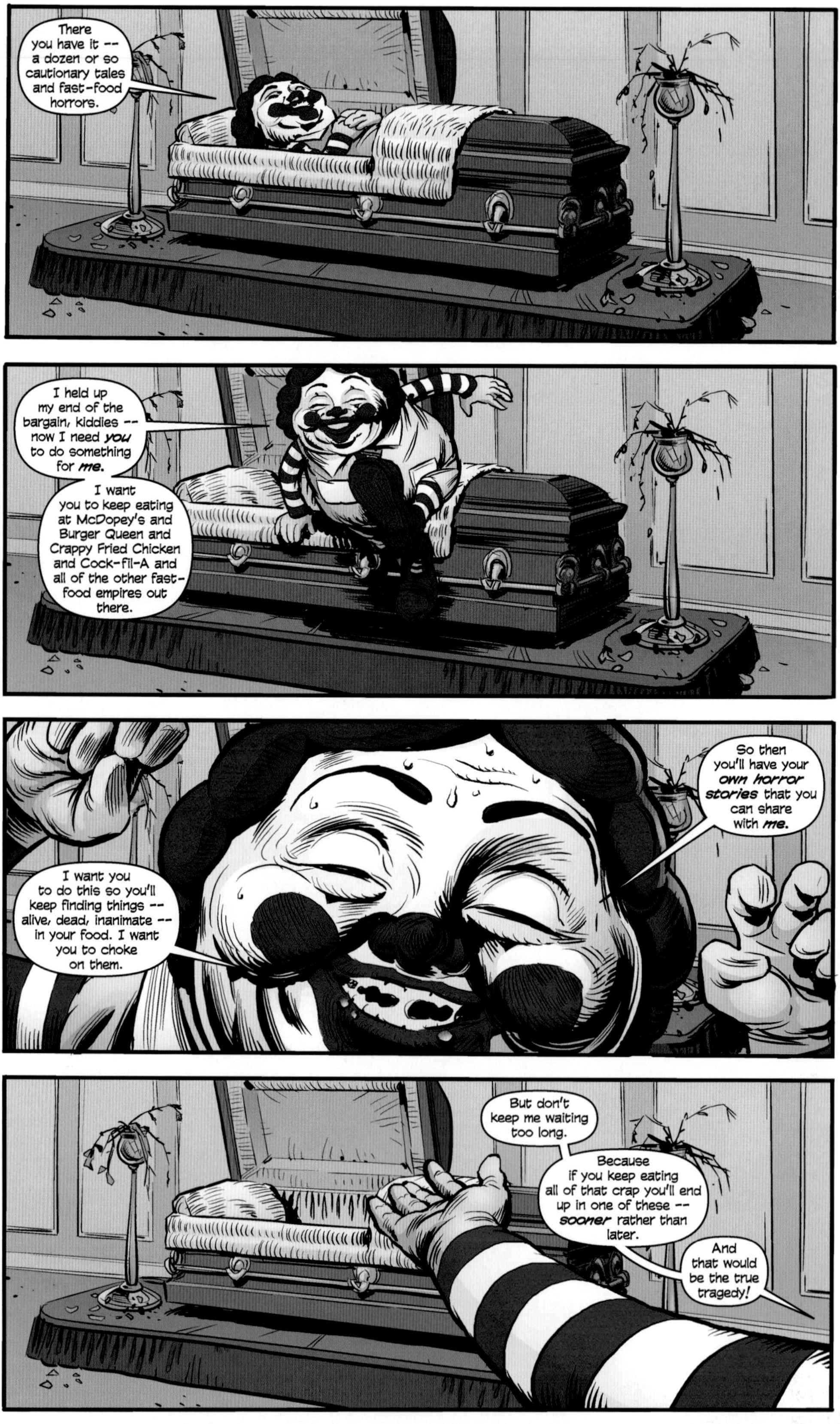
There you have it -- a dozen or so cautionary tales and fast-food horrors.
I held up my end of the bargain, kiddies -- now I need *you* to do something for *me*.
I want you to keep eating at McDopey's and Burger Queen and Crappy Fried Chicken and Cock-fil-A and all of the other fast-food empires out there.
I want you to do this so you'll keep finding things -- alive, dead, inanimate -- in your food. I want you to choke on them.
So then you'll have your *own horror stories* that you can share with *me*.
But don't keep me waiting too long.
Because if you keep eating all of that crap you'll end up in one of these -- *sooner* rather than later.
And that would be the true tragedy!

Talent is no substitute for taste.

Ron English

popaganda.com